SALVATION COMES FROM THE LORD

SALVATION COMES FROM THE LORD

ARNOLD VALENTIN WALLENKAMPF

Review and Herald Publishing Association
Washington, DC 20039-0555
Hagerstown, MD 21740

Texts of Scripture quoted in this book, unless otherwise indicated, are from *The Holy Bible: New International Version*. Copyright © 1978 by the New York International Bible Society. Used by permission of Zondervan Bible Publishers.

Other versions used, besides the King James Version (K.J.V.), are as follows:

Bible texts credited to Amplified are from *The Amplified Bible and New Testament*. Copyright 1965 by the Lockman Foundation. Used by permission.

Bible texts credited to Barclay are from *The New Testament*, William Barclay, translator. William Collins Sons & Co., Ltd., New York, publishers. Used by permission.

Bible texts credited to Jerusalem are from *The Jerusalem Bible*, copyright © 1966 by Darton, Longman & Todd, Ltd., and Doubleday & Company, Inc. Used by permission of the publishers.

Bible texts credited to Moffatt are from *The Bible: A New Translation* by James Moffatt. Copyright by James Moffatt 1954. Used by permission of Harper & Row, Publishers, Incorporated.

Scripture quotations credited to N.A.S.B. are from the *New American Standard Bible*, © The Lockman Foundation 1960, 1962, 1963, 1968, 1971, 1972, 1973, 1975, and are used by permission.

Bible texts credited to N.E.B. are from *The New English Bible*. © The Delegates of the Oxford University Press and the Syndics of the Cambridge University Press 1961, 1970. Reprinted by permission.

Bible texts credited to Phillips are from J. B. Phillips: *The New Testament in Modern English*, Revised Edition © J. B. Phillips 1958, 1960, 1962. Used by permission of The Macmillan Publishing Co., Inc.

The Scripture quotations marked R.S.V. are from the Revised Standard Version of the Bible, copyrighted 1946, 1952 © 1971, 1973.

Bible texts credited to T.E.V. are from the *Good News Bible*—Old Testament: Copyright © American Bible Society 1976; New Testament: Copyright © American Bible Society 1966, 1971, 1976.

Verses marked T.L.B. are taken from *The Living Bible*, copyright 1971 by Tyndale House Publishers, Wheaton, Ill. Used by permission.

Printed in U.S.A.

Library of Congress Cataloging in Publication Data

Wallenkampf, Arnold Valentin, 1913-
Salvation comes from the Lord.

Includes bibliographical references.
1. Salvation. 2. Bible. N.T. Galatians—Criticism, interpretation, etc. 3. Bible. N.T. James—Criticism, interpretation, etc. I. Title.
BT751.2.W36 1983 234 83-3297
ISBN 0-8280-0210-X

Contents

Introduction

This book briefly discusses the way of salvation, the how and by what means men and women dead in sin can be made spiritually alive and fit for heavenly society.

Before Jesus left His disciples, He told them that He was going away to prepare a place for them, and then He would return to take them, and all His followers, to live with Him forever. But when Jesus comes for His own, He will not veil His divinity with humanity the way He did the first time. He will appear as King of kings and Lord of lords. To sinners, His very appearance at that time will be a consuming fire.

The question then arises, How or by what means will sinners be able to meet Him in His divine glory and live in His presence? We will draw our answer mainly from two New Testament Epistles: Paul's Epistle to the Galatians and the book of James.

But who were the Galatians? Two theories attempt to identify the audience of Paul's Galatian Epistle: the South Galatian and the North Galatian theory.

The South Galatian theory maintains that the apostle wrote the Epistle to believers in the southern part of the Roman province of Galatia. Paul and

Barnabas raised up churches at Pisidian Antioch, Iconium, Lystra, and Derbe during Paul's first missionary journey. The North Galatian theory holds that its recipients were ethnic Galatians Paul and Silas had won to Christianity in the northern part of the province.

Luke does not designate the region where Paul and Barnabas evangelized as Galatia. But on Paul's Second Missionary Tour, Luke specifically mentions their entering Galatia after traversing the regions visited by Paul and Barnabas. "Thus it seems probable that after visiting Derbe, Lystra, Iconium, and other cities of Lycaonia (Acts 16:1-4; cf. chap. 14:6 . . .), Paul's company went westward into Phrygia, and northward into a region that was locally known as Galatia. In both areas they would preach the good news to the heathen inhabitants, and thus establish groups of believers that developed into the Galatian churches."[1]

Ellen G. White comments that "having visited the churches in Pisidia and the neighboring region, Paul and Silas, with Timothy, pressed on into 'Phrygia and the region of Galatia,' where with mighty power they proclaimed the glad tidings of salvation."[2]

The Galatians "had never before known of the true God."[3] Paul and his colaborers were the first to teach them "the fundamental truths concerning 'God the Father' and 'our Lord Jesus Christ, who gave himself for our sins, that he might deliver us from this present evil world, according to the will of God and our Father.'"[4]

The thesis of Galatians is basically the same as that of Romans, about which Ellen G. White states: "Through all the ages the great truth of justification by faith has stood as a mighty beacon to guide repentant sinners into the way of life. It was this light that scattered the darkness which enveloped Luther's mind and revealed to him the power of the blood of Christ to cleanse from sin. The same light has guided thousands of sin-burdened souls to the true Source of pardon and peace."[5]

For Luther the teaching of justification by faith broke the oppressive yoke of vainly seeking to find peace with God and surety of salvation by observing the rituals imposed on him by the monastic system. The liberating light first dawned on him as he read the book of Galatians. As a result, Galatians became exceedingly precious to Luther. It opened to him the gateway to freedom from the crushing burden of sin and offered comfort and joy in Christian living. "The Epistle to the Galatians is my epistle, to which I am betrothed," he said. "It is my Katie von Bora."[6] It became as loved and indispensable to him as his wife, Katie. He depended on it for his knowledge and surety of salvation.

While the Epistle to the Galatians teaches salvation by grace through justification by faith, that of James appears to make salvation result from personal activity, or works. Luther's dismissal of James as an "epistle of straw"[7] has unfortunately colored the attitude of most Protestants down to our own time. They have forgotten his further remarks that "I praise it and consider it a good book, because it sets up no doctrines of men but vigorously promulgates the law of God" and that "in a word, he [James] wanted to guard against those who relied on faith without works."[8]

The two Epistles, Galatians and James, are totally different. The apostle Paul, God's chosen instrument to present the gospel to the Gentiles, addressed Galatians to Gentile Christians. James wrote to Jewish Christians. Paul unabashedly teaches justification and salvation by grace through faith in Jesus Christ. James, on the other hand, has been accused of teaching justification by works.

Consequently many have regarded Paul's Epistle to the Galatians and James's Epistle as contradicting each other. In the succeeding pages we shall briefly examine this problem.

[1] *The Seventh-day Adventist Bible Commentary* (Washington, D.C.: Review and Herald Pub. Assn., 1957), vol. 6, p. 337.

[2] Ellen G. White, *The Acts of the Apostles* (Mountain View, Calif.: Pacific Press Pub. Assn., 1911), p. 207.

[3] *Ibid.*, pp. 207, 208.

[4] *Ibid.*, p. 208.

[5] *Ibid.*, pp. 373, 374.

[6] Jaroslav Pelikan (ed.), *Luther's Works* (St. Louis: Concordia Pub. House, 1963), vol. 26, p. ix.

[7] Ewald M. Plass (comp.), *What Luther Says* (St. Louis: Concordia Pub. House, 1959), Vol. II, p. 988.

[8] Helmut T. Lehmann (ed.), *Luther's Works* (Philadelphia: Muhlenberg Press, 1960), vol. 35, pp. 395, 397.

Salvation Comes From the Lord

No person has ever succeeded in doing everything right. Rather, everyone has sensed disappointment or chagrin over some mistake or shortcoming. Each of us has been aware of having failed to live up both to our own hopes and the expectations of others.

In teaching religion, I at times had quibblers in class. Bright and mentally alert students raised, for the sheer fun of it, some facetiously specious question or proposition to see what my answer might be. When the hairsplitting continued longer than I thought appropriate, I would comment, "Some day we shall all stand before the judgment seat of God. There will be no quibbling then. But even today most of us know deep down in our heart what is right and what is wrong. On that day we shall all be judged by what we have known."

The disturbance in class then always subsided. The courts of their own inner selves—their consciences—convicted the previously bantering students.

All of us are sinners, and "the wages of sin is death" (Rom. 6:23), because there is no life apart from God. He is its only source in the entire universe. When we sin or depart from Him, we run away from life. The wise man declared, " 'But he who sins against me injures himself; all those who hate me love death' " (Prov. 8:36, N.A.S.B.).

Adam and Eve started it. They introduced sin to our world by eating the forbidden fruit, and they hid from God in the ancient Garden. They were not alone in sin. Isaiah spoke for each one of us when he said, "We all, like sheep, have gone astray, each of us has turned to his own way" (Isa. 53:6). "But your iniquities have separated you from your God; your sins have hidden his face from you, so that he will not hear" (chap. 59:2). The New Testament presents the same witness: "For all have sinned and fall short of the glory of God" (Rom. 3:23).

It is not only the bad people—thieves and harlots, liars and dissemblers, and other derelicts—who have turned away from God and require salvation. All of us need it.

Other than Jesus Christ, the good and upright people mentioned in the Bible were all sinners. Daniel was one of them, although the heavenly messenger addressed him, "O Daniel, you greatly beloved man" (Dan. 10:11, Amplified).

A remarkable man, Daniel as a youth was one of a group of four Hebrews selected for special education and training to serve the Babylonian king as civil servants (chap. 1:4). The leader among his fellow captives, he petitioned the official responsible for the four of them for a vegetarian diet rather than the meat coming from the king's table (verses 12, 8).

Although all four youths excelled in their studies (verse 20), Daniel also understood "visions and dreams of all kinds" (verse 17). His special endowment brought him to the attention of Nebuchadnezzar and later his grandson Belshazzar (chaps. 2:24-28; 5:11-17).

Darius, the conquering Mede, also discovered Daniel's talent and usefulness and planned to make him his deputy (chap. 6:3). Besides, "Daniel was a devoted servant of the Most High. His long life was filled up with noble deeds of service for his Master. His purity of character and unwavering fidelity are equaled only by his humility of heart and his contrition before God."[1]

But although men especially esteemed Daniel, and Heaven loved him, he was still a sinner. Approaching God in prayer, he confessed his sins (chap. 9:20) and "trusted in his God" (chap. 6:23). He did not rely on his own righteousness, but on God's forgiveness of sin (chap. 9:19) and His gift of salvation and eternal life.

Nicodemus too was an upright man, possessing both learning and position. He was a Pharisee, a member of a Jewish sect strictly orthodox and deeply concerned with the preservation of the purity of the Jewish religion. If anyone should merit salvation, Nicodemus certainly should have. But Jesus startled him by saying, "'I tell you the truth, unless a man is born of water and the Spirit, he cannot enter the kingdom of God. Flesh gives birth to flesh, but the Spirit gives birth to spirit. You should not be surprised at my saying, "You must be born again"'" (John 3:5-7).

Nicodemus, in his impeccable Pharisaic righteousness, was not fit for the kingdom of God. He needed to humble himself and be born again through the Holy Spirit to become a child of God.

The rich young ruler approached Christ, "and Jesus looking upon him loved him" (Mark 10:21, R.S.V.). Although loved by Him and God the Father Himself, he was still lost for eternity as he walked away. What could possibly withhold salvation from a person whom Jesus, the Saviour of the world, loved as He did that young man? Jesus longed to save him.

But salvation does not depend solely on God's love for us. If it did, then universalism, or the belief that all will ultimately be saved, would be correct. Thus some even believe that Satan will be saved in the end.[2] Jesus truly loved Satan and the fallen angels. He did not want them to be lost. But they are because they refused to respond to His love.

God loves everyone born into the world, and " 'his love endures forever' " (1 Chron. 16:41), "because God is love" (1 John 4:8). We need have no question about it. Because God loves us, He sent His Son to this earth. " 'For God so loved the world that he gave his one and only Son, that whoever believes in him shall not perish but have eternal life' " (John 3:16). He also loved the people of Jerusalem and said that He longed to bring her " 'children together, as a hen gathers her chicks under her wings, but you were not willing' " (Matt. 23:37). Hence he could not save them.

No person will necessarily forfeit eternal life because he is a sinner or has sinned. While all of us are sinners and have sinned, every person may be freed from the sentence of death. However, in order to escape eternal death, we must respond to God's love and ask for deliverance.

In August, 1979, the American authorities detained a Soviet jet at Kennedy Airport in New York to give the ballerina Ludmila Vlasova, the wife of the defected Moscow-based Bolshoi Ballet star Alexander Godunov, a chance to request political asylum in the United States, if she chose to remain with her husband. Grim-faced Soviet diplomats and police agents had escorted her up the ramp of the Aeroflot plane after holding her at the Mayflower Hotel for two days. Then Soviet officials refused her permission to come to a room adjacent to the plane "where she could see for herself that she is free to go or stay." On board the Aeroflot jet in the presence of Soviet officials she said that she wanted to return home rather than defect with her husband.[3]

Had the ballerina, on the other hand, expressed a desire to remain in the United States with her husband, the American authorities would have immediately honored her request. But she did not do so. Consequently the Aeroflot plane finally left, after days of delay, with her and the other ballet dancers for the Soviet Union. She chose not to use her opportunity to defect.

The United States security men would and could not take her off the plane unless she indicated she wanted to remain in America. If they had done so without her spoken request, the Russians would have accused them of violating her free choice.

God is in the same position before the universe as the United States security men were in that situation. If He saved anyone against his or her expressed will, other beings would view it as disregarding the person's free will and choice.

God gave Adam and Eve free moral choice at their creation. They used it to eat the fruit of the tree of the knowledge of good and evil in the Garden of Eden. Men and women have often since employed their remarkable faculty of free moral choice contrary to God's will. And God has not removed it. Free moral choice is yours and mine. It is God's inalienable gift to every human being.

Our salvation pivots on our free moral choice. Salvation demands that you and I—and every intelligent being on earth—must personally choose to respond to God's love in order to be saved.

God appeals to the sinner to opt for salvation. " 'Here I am!' " Jesus says. " 'I stand at the door and knock. If anyone hears my voice and opens the door, I will go in and eat with him, and he with me' " (Rev. 3:20). "The Spirit and the bride say, 'Come!' And let him who hears say, 'Come!' Whoever is thirsty, let him come; and whoever wishes, let him take the free gift of the water of life" (chap. 22:17). If we ask Him, God will save us. "It is a part of God's plan to grant us, in answer to the prayer of faith, that which He would not bestow did we not thus ask."[4]

When a man wants to marry a girl, he tells her he loves her and asks her to marry him. However, the marriage does not depend on his desire to marry her, but upon whether she responds to his proposal. Without her acceptance, there will be no marriage, regardless of how ardently he loves her and wants her to be his wife. Ultimately it is her decision, not his, that counts.

So it is with God's desire to save us. If we do not open ourselves to God's overtures of love, He cannot save us, in spite of His undying love for us. The prodigal's return to his father's house illustrates salvation. The father loved the wandering son all the time, and sorrow had filled him when the lad walked away from home. His heart went out in love for the son all the time he was in the foreign country. But the father's love did not control his offspring's free moral choice. Not until " 'he came to his senses' " (Luke 15:17) and responded to his parent's searching love could the son exchange his old tattered clothes for the beautiful garment the father gave him.

A person sentenced to death cannot himself save his life. But an executive pardon can. By having sinned, you and I find ourselves condemned to death. "If you bore the guilt of your sin, it would crush you; but the sinless One has taken your place."[5] The only hope of salvation with eternal life is an executive pardon by the Ruler of the universe. He is eager to grant it if we acclaim Jesus as our Saviour.

A couple of decades ago a young man in the Midwest lost his temper and wound up in a fight with his brother, beating him so unmercifully that the latter finally died. The court condemned the murderer to death. But all the neighbors, remembering him as a good man, reasoned that the terrible incident was just a single slip. They appealed to the governor to pardon him, and he responded favorably.

But before he would pardon the murderer, he dressed as a minister and went to the prison to see the young man. However, the convict did not want to speak to the alleged minister, and told him to leave him alone. Silently the governor departed. Soon afterward the warden came to visit the prisoner and asked how he and the governor had gotten along.

"What do you mean, the governor?" the murderer demanded.

"Yes, the governor. He was just here to see you."

"You mean that preacher was the governor?"

"Yes, he was the governor," the warden answered.

Spurned by the convicted man, the governor went back to his office. Later one of the prisoner's former neighbors called on him and inquired, "What are you going to do with the young man condemned to death?"

"That case is closed," the official told him. Then he explained that he had gone to the prison to talk to him, and that the prisoner had refused to speak to him and told him to go away.

The day of the execution came. The warden granted the young man the privilege of making a statement if he so desired. "Let it never be said that I die because I killed my brother," the murderer said. "I die because I rejected the governor and his pardon."

So it is with us. No one will ever forfeit eternal life because of Adam's sin or his own, however heinous. But everyone who dies the eternal death will do so because he has refused to accept Jesus as his Saviour and be saved from sin.

Our only hope of salvation is to receive it as a gift from God through Jesus. The morally good rich young ruler whom Jesus loved rejected it. Dante may have referred to him in his *Inferno* when he wrote, "And when I'd noted here and there a shade whose face I knew, I saw and recognized the coward spirit of the man who made the great refusal."[6] Daniel and Nicodemus were also sinners, and probably no better morally than the young man who had kept all the commandments since he was a boy (Mark 10:20). In the eyes of man he was an exemplary youth, but in the gaze of God he was a sinner like you and me, desperately in need of salvation.

Salvation Comes From the Lord

As Jesus taught in the parable of the man without a wedding garment (Matt. 22:1-14), no human being can furnish his own wedding garment. Salvation can come only as a gift. "For it is by grace you have been saved, through faith—and this not from yourselves, it is the gift of God—not by works, so that no one can boast" (Eph. 2:8, 9). "The gift of God is eternal life in Christ Jesus our Lord" (Rom. 6:23). If we choose to be justified and saved, we must receive both justification and salvation as gifts, for " 'salvation comes from the Lord' " (Jonah 2:9).

---

[1] Ellen G. White, *The Sanctified Life* (Washington, D.C.: Review and Herald Pub. Assn., 1937), p. 52.

[2] Just before probation closes, "Satan himself is converted, after the modern order of things," Ellen G. White writes in *The Great Controversy* (Mountain View, Calif.: Pacific Press Pub. Assn., 1911), page 588.

[3] Donald McHenry, Deputy U.S. Ambassador at the United Nations, in *Time*, Sept. 3, 1979, p. 28.

[4] White, *The Great Controversy*, p. 525.

[5] Ellen G. White, in *Signs of the Times*, April 9, 1894.

[6] *Inferno*, III, 58-60.

Saving Faith

Faith in God is indispensable for salvation, for "without faith it is impossible to please God, because anyone who comes to him must believe that he exists and that he rewards those who earnestly seek him" (Heb. 11:6). But what constitutes saving faith? We use the word *faith* to denote so many different attitudes toward both things, persons, and God. It has almost as indefinite a meaning as the word *love.*

Possibly the best way to ascertain the meaning of faith with reference to God might be to look at some of the people in the Bible who possessed saving faith and notice how they related to Him and His will.

We start with Abraham. He is "called God's friend" (James 2:23). Genuine friendship presupposes mutual confidence and trust—faith. Abraham trusted God. "By faith Abraham, when called to go to a place he would later receive as his inheritance, obeyed and went, even though he did not know where he was going. By faith he made his home in the promised land like a stranger in a foreign country; he lived in tents" (Heb. 11:8, 9).

At the time of God's initial summons Abraham resided at Ur in Chaldea, on the west bank of the

Euphrates River not far from the Persian Gulf. Although wealthy in both cattle and land, he was disturbed by his neighbors who scorned his belief in the true God. He wanted to find a place where he could worship without either contempt or annoyance. In search of such a land he went with his father, Terah, to Haran (Acts 7:2-4). When he was 75 years old God asked him to leave even Haran and journey to a land that He would show him (Gen. 12:1). Again Abraham obeyed, and the Lord guided him to Canaan.

"Abraham's unquestioning obedience is one of the most striking evidences of faith to be found in all the Bible. To him, faith was 'the substance of things hoped for, the evidence of things not seen.' Relying upon the divine promise, without the least outward assurance of its fulfillment, he abandoned home and kindred and native land, and went forth, he knew not whither, to follow where God should lead."[1]

But Abraham's faith in God was not always unwavering. Having trusted God to protect him and his household on his journey across the Syrian Desert and among strangers in Canaan, Abraham failed to have faith in God's protective care in Egypt (verses 10-13) and later on in Gerar (chap. 20:1-13). In both instances he resorted to lying, inferring that Sarah was not his wife, but only his sister. It was a half truth, because she was his half sister, the daughter of his father, but not of his mother (verse 12). Nevertheless in saying that Sarah was his sister he deliberately intended to deceive, and "an intention to deceive is what constitutes falsehood."[2]

But Abraham surmounted his weakness in faith. When the supreme test came to him to sacrifice his only son Isaac, he did not waver, but did exactly what God asked of him (chap. 22:1-14). By that time Abraham's faith had grown so strong that he believed that God would even raise a sacrificed Isaac from the dead (Heb. 11:19), if need be, to grant him "descendants as numerous as the stars in the sky and as the sand on the seashore" (Gen. 22:17). In this way "God's friend" became also known as "the father of all who believe" (Rom. 4:11).

Samuel illustrates a child's faith and loyalty to God. Hannah, his mother, gave her boy to God by bringing him to the tabernacle as she had promised before his birth (1 Sam. 1:11). The evil example of Eli's sons (chap. 2:12-17) did not make it an ideal place for an impressionable youth to grow in loyalty to God. But in spite of their sinful lives, "the boy Samuel continued to grow in stature and in favor with the Lord and with men" (verse 26).

During Samuel's earliest childhood years at home his mother implanted in his receptive mind lessons for eternity. Sometimes we assume that a child is too young to know and give his heart to God and maintain a living relationship with Him. That is wrong. He or she can be just as wholehearted and honest in his commitment to God and His will as an adult—perhaps even more so. Adults often operate from a bundle of mixed motives. Most children are more simple and uncomplicated in their responses. Trusting, they do not weigh every possible consequence of their deeds, but are immediate and direct. They harbor no suspicion, doubts, or worries. Their faith is complete. Jesus said that " 'the kingdom of heaven belongs to such as these' " (Matt. 19:14). Age is apparently no prerequisite for knowing God as a friend and Jesus as one's Saviour.

The boy Samuel was committed to God and served Him with a child's full devotion. As a result of his attitude of openness to God, the Lord could speak to him when He could not communicate to the high priest and his associates, His official representatives (1 Sam. 3:1, 4, 6, 10, 11). Young Samuel possessed saving faith.

While Moses was herding his father-in-law's sheep in Midian the story of Job came to his attention. He recorded it, and it became one of the oldest books of the Bible.[3]

Job was a renowed sheik in the land of Uz, possessing land and large herds of cattle. He and his wife also had a family of seven sons and three daughters. But sudden calamity befell them. Their children perished in a natural catastrophe, and raiding bedouins from the desert stole the cattle after attacking and killing the herdsmen. Shortly afterward a loathesome disease struck Job himself. His wife lost her faith in God. She wanted her husband also to renounce his faith in God and told him, " 'Curse God and die!' " (Job 2:9).

Most of Job's friends—who previously had looked up to him—now forsook him in the moment of his greatest need. The four who did not accused him of secret sins as the cause of his misfortunes. In the face of all of it Job maintained his innocence before God; yet he also attributed his ill fate to Him (chaps. 10:3; 13:15; 19:9, 21; 27:2; 30:11, 19).

But as a child trusts his parents, even though he may not understand their doings, so Job trusted God, even though he did not comprehend His ways. He vowed, "Though he slay me, yet will I trust in him: but I will maintain mine own ways before him" (chap. 13:15), K.J.V.). Confidently he looked forward to the resurrection when he would see God face to face. " 'And after my skin has been destroyed, yet in my flesh I will see God; I myself will see him with my own eyes—I, and not another. How my heart yearns within me!' " (chap. 19:26, 27).

Perhaps Mary, the mother of Jesus, manifested the most implicit example of faith, or trust, in God, in the Bible. When the angel Gabriel appeared to her and told her that she would bear a Son, although she was a virgin, she did not argue or remonstrate. " 'I am the Lord's servant,' Mary answered. 'May it be to me as you have said' " (Luke 1:38).

Wholly God's, she willingly surrendered herself "'body and soul'" (verse 38, Phillips) to Him and was prepared and eager to be and do anything He chose for her. She held back nothing, not even refusing to become pregnant without a husband, even though the Jews considered it a great disgrace. Both she and her Son, Jesus, were in later life taunted for his allegedly illegitimate birth, while His Jewish slanderers prided themselves that they were "'not illegitimate children'" (John 8:41), as they inferred He was.

Mary trusted God and believed that He knew what was best for both her and His kingdom, and that He had power to bring about the humanly impossible. Willingly she would let Him use her in any way He saw best, in contrast to the "righteous" (Luke 1:6, K.J.V.) priest Zacharias, who doubted God's ability to give him a son in his old age. Although he knew his people's history, that Abraham had received a son by Sarah when they were old, doubts arose in his mind when he thought of his and Elizabeth's advanced age.

On a journey to the region of Phoenicia, or present-day Lebanon, Jesus and His disciples met a woman who implored Him to heal her sick daughter. At first Jesus pretended not to notice her, and His disciples, believing her to be a pest, asked Him to "'send her away, for she keeps crying out after us'" (Matt. 15:23). When Jesus told her that He had not come to help pagans, but only Israelites, and that children's food should not be given to dogs, His seeming rudeness did not offend her. "Pride and prejudice meant nothing to her, and she would not let these deter her."[4] Believing that Jesus could and wanted to help her, she retained "irrepressible trust in Him whose face and tones so contradicted His words."[5] "Beneath the apparent refusal of Jesus, she saw a compassion that He could not hide."[6]

Ignoring Jesus' apparent brushoff, she persisted in her plea for help. Finally Jesus acknowledged her faith by saying, " 'Woman, you have great faith! Your request is granted' " (verse 28).

Faith evidently does not always manifest itself in the same way in all believers. In the case of Abraham it meant taking God at His word both when He requested him to leave his native land and when He asked him to sacrifice his only son of promise, Isaac. But that would have been a disaster and not faith at all in the case of the Syrophoenician woman. If she had taken Jesus at His word, she would promptly and disgustedly have left Him when He so apparently callously and rudely responded to her plea for help. But she held on to her confidence in Him. She trusted Jesus in spite of His "unkind" words, believing that He both could and wanted to help her and do her good.

Job's faith demonstrated itself in still another way. When calamity and physical suffering overtook him, he was puzzled and did not understand what was happening to him. In his failure to understand the cause of his misfortune, he impugned God for bringing trials upon him. And in a way he was right. His problem was that he failed to differentiate between what God actively does and what He passively permits. The Lord did allow Satan to afflict Job, that His confidence in Job's integrity might be vindicated. God dared subject Job to this test because he knew he would pass it successfully and thus refute Satan's charge that the man served him only because of ulterior motives (Job 1:9-11).

Despite his perplexity, Job's faith in God was like that of the mature Abraham, "who against hope believed in hope" (Rom. 4:18, K.J.V.) that God would even raise Isaac from the dead. Also, Job's faith reflected that of Jesus when on the cross He cried out, " 'My God, my God, why have you forsaken me?' " (Matt. 27:46), yet in His dying moment committed His fate to Him (see Luke 23:46). Confidently Job said that " 'I know I will be vindicated' " (Job 13:18), although it might not be until the final judgment.

Job's confidence in God did not depend on his being showered with continuous blessings of physical well-being, financial prosperity, and acceptance and popularity among his peers and neighbors. The patriarch's philosophy of life included adversity as well as prosperity, and his faith made room for both personal destitution and physical suffering.

The Holy Spirit had done His homework in Job's heart. Therefore he could answer his wife when she chided him for his faithfulness to God despite overwhelming personal catastrophe, "'Shall we accept good from God, and not trouble?'" (chap. 2:10). His trust in the Lord's justice went beyond the present. He believed that God was testing him, but "'when he has tested me, I will come forth as gold'" (chap 23:10). Thus he looked forward with confidence to the resurrection.

"Sooner or later," Leslie Weatherhead noted, "everybody needs a faith or a philosophy of life big enough and strong enough to stand up to disaster. Blessed is he who has his anchor secure before the storm breaks. When what we call disaster breaks upon us, we are too stunned to be able to arrange our ideas, too bewildered to begin to erect our faith." Luther said that "if someone passes through evil with a courageous and happy spirit, then the Holy Spirit has already performed His work in him."[7]

God would not have dared to present the tests He gave to Abraham and Job to many people. "Difficulties are God's errands," Henry Ward Beecher wrote, "and when we are sent upon them we should esteem it a proof of God's confidence." In asking Abraham to sacrifice Isaac, God dispatched him on a terrible errand. The same was true of Job amid extreme adversity, and the Syrophoenician woman to whom Jesus spoke so "rudely." God had confidence in them.

Shortly after World War II, I had a student at Union College who had just come back from the European theater of the war. His induction into the Army had occurred immediately after his conversion. In the fervor of his newfound faith he went to Europe and became a participant in some of the fiercest engagements of the war, such as the Salerno beach invasion of fortress Europe. Once he told us in class that even though his comrades were falling all around him, he knew that God would protect him. "I had the promise," he said, "of Psalm 91:7 that 'a thousand may fall at your side, ten thousand at your right hand, but it will not come near you.'"

Responding to his implicit but immature confidence in God's protective care, I told him, "Your faith was good enough to live by, but it was not good enough to die by. What would have happened to your faith in God if you had been mortally wounded and faced death?"

As God's children in the sunset hours of earth's history, we shall by His grace develop a faith and trust in Him that will enable us to accept both adversity and good days. We will have a faith enabling us to die for Him if need be—as well as live for Him in opulence and comfort. "Those who would rather die than perform a wrong act are the only ones who will be found faithful."[8] "It is better to die than to sin; better to want than to defraud; better to hunger than to lie."[9]

"Faith is the confident and receptive mind, humbling itself that it may be filled with truth; faith is the loyal and adoring heart, giving itself that it may find divine communion; faith is the active and obedient will, surrendering itself that it may know true righteousness."[10] "Faith is trusting God—believing that He loves us and knows best what is for our good."[11] "Faith in Jesus Christ . . . is the act of the soul by which the whole man is given over to the guardianship and control of Jesus Christ. He abides in Christ and Christ abides in the soul by faith as supreme. The believer commits his soul and body to God. . . . There will be an assurance that the soul is washed in the blood of Christ and clothed with His righteousness and precious in the sight of Jesus."[12] This is saving faith.

But the Bible also speaks of dead faith. The apostle James elaborates on such pseudo faith. In chapter 2 of his Epistle he points out that if the believers have saving faith they will not display partiality to the rich over the poor (see verses 1-13). True faith will motivate them to act as Jesus did, even toward the poor.

He goes on to show that saving faith will lead the believers to give food and clothing to the poor, rather than just to express a wish that they might be fed and clothed (verses 14-16). Faith that produces no action, he says, is dead (verse 17). Even the devils possess such faith, he comments (see verse 19).

He contrasts pseudo faith, which is actionless, with saving faith, which inevitably prompts to activity. Abraham and Rahab exemplify the latter—Abraham when he prepared to sacrifice his son Isaac, and Rahab when she saved the Israelite spies (verses 20-26). Of Abraham, James states "that by these actions the integrity of his faith was fully proved" (verse 22, N.E.B.). His response testified to the soundness of his faith.

Saving faith and works, or deeds, are tied together. They cannot exist separately. Abraham, Samuel, Moses, Job, Mary, and the Syrophoenician woman—all possessed saving faith. It led them to trust God and act accordingly.

---

[1] Ellen G. White, *Patriarchs and Prophets* (Mountain View, Calif.: Pacific Press Pub. Assn., 1958), p. 126.

[2] *Ibid.*, p. 309.

[3] See Ellen G. White, *Education* (Mountain View, Calif.: Pacific Press Pub. Assn., 1952), p. 159.

[4] *The SDA Bible Commentary* (Washington, D.C.: Review and Herald Pub. Assn., 1956), vol. 5, pp. 421, 422.

[5] Cunningham Geikie, *The Life and Words of Christ* (New York: D. Appleton and Company, 1882), Vol. II, p. 219.

[6] Ellen G. White, *The Desire of Ages* (Mountain View, Calif.: Pacific Press Pub. Assn., 1940), p. 401.

[7] Jaroslav Pelikan (ed.), *Luther's Works*, vol. 26, p. 384.

[8] Ellen G. White, *Testimonies* (Mountain View, Calif.: Pacific Press Pub. Assn., 1948), vol. 5, p. 53.

[9] *Ibid.*, vol. 4, p. 495.

[10] From O. F. Blackwelder, in *The Interpreter's Bible*, vol. 10, p. 546. Used by permission of Abingdon Press.

[11] White, *Education*, p. 253.

[12] Ellen G. White, *Mind, Character, and Personality* (Nashville: Southern Pub. Assn., 1977), vol. 2, p. 531.

The Beginnings of Paul's Missionary Activities

Saul received his call to evangelism from God Himself (Acts 26:16-18). But in spite of his divine commission, he did not demand that the pillars of the Jerusalem church, including Peter and James, should recognize and accept him as an evangelist. On his first postconversion visit to Jerusalem they gave him no commission to evangelize, but sent him off to his native Tarsus, apparently to be forgotten. There he remained, "unknown by sight to the churches of Judea" (Gal. 1:22, N.A.S.B.). When the growth of the church at Antioch in Syria became too great for Barnabas to handle, he went to Tarsus to find Saul and solicit his help.

At Antioch the Holy Spirit prompted the leaders of the church to set aside Barnabas and Saul for the work to which God had called them (Acts 13:2), confirming Saul's divine call to the ministry. Having been commissioned by the leaders of the church at Antioch for the work among the Gentiles, Barnabas and Saul prepared to begin their missionary activities, accompanied by young John Mark as helper. But where?

Saul submitted his travel plans to the Spirit's guidance. The apostle never traveled as a gypsy or as freakish impulse would prompt, but always with purpose. Later in his ministry, revelation led him to the Jerusalem Council (Gal. 2:1, 2), turned him away from the Roman provinces of Asia and Bithynia to Troas, and beckoned him toward Macedonia (Acts 16:6-10). Saul not only was a member of the early Christian church, but also passed the acid test for being a genuine son of God, being "led by the Spirit of God" (Rom. 8:14). He submitted his travel plans to God, to carry out or give up as His providence would indicate. Without a doubt, as Barnabas and Saul set sail for Cyprus, Barnabas' homeland (Acts 4:36), the Spirit directed them.

We do not know their route across the island of Cyprus from Salamis to Paphos. Scholars have variously suggested the southern route through Citium, the northern through Soli, and the central one over the mountain range. Nor does Scripture tell us how much they preached as they went. At the provincial capital of Paphos the proconsul, Sergius Paulus, sent for them "because he wanted to hear the word of God" (chap. 13:7). A Jewish sorcerer, Elymas, resisted Barnabas and Saul, and the Lord, at the apostle's request, smote him with temporary blindness, converting the governor and winning for Christianity a great victory (verses 6-12). "In passing, it is interesting to observe that Saul is first called Paul in connection with the interview with the governor. This was his first significant Gentile contact and the first use of his Greek name." [1] From here on Luke calls him Paul, and Paul becomes the leader of the traveling party.

At Paphos the missionaries boarded ship for Pamphylia in Asia Minor, passing up the river Cestrus to Perga (verse 13). From Perga, John Mark returned to Jerusalem. Choosing to continue their journey on land, Paul and Barnabas traveled north, the only option open to them. No roads and no population centers edged the Mediterranean in southern Asia Minor. "Along the entire length of the southern seaboard of Asia Minor, the mountains descend steeply to the sea, except in the regions of Pamphylia and eastern Cilicia."[2]

So from Perga, Paul and Barnabas made the hundred-mile trek north to Pisidian Antioch, at an altitude of 3,600 feet. This city was situated near a trade route from Ephesus to the East. After traversing the Maeander Valley, passing through Laodicea, Colossae, and Apamea, the road they followed came to Pisidian Antioch. Then it dropped south, touching Iconium, Lystra, and Derbe before turning east toward the Cilician Gates and down to Tarsus.

In his missionary journeys Paul made a point of visiting districts and places readily available by ancient trade routes. These places probably also had large Jewish colonies. He knew the Jewish Diaspora, or Dispersion, himself belonging to it.

Some Jews from the Dispersion settled in Jerusalem. Synagogues arose there whose congregations consisted of foreign Jews, those from the same area grouping together. There was probably a synagogue of Cilicians and those from Asia Minor to which the young Saul may have belonged during his days as a student under Gamaliel. Also, he made acquaintances that became valuable connections for his future—but then undreamed-of—journeys. From such friends he probably also learned of the current geographic distribution of Jews along the travel routes of the Roman Empire. Friendship connections, as well as family and tribal ties, most likely helped to shape his travels.

Except during his visits to Galatia and Phrygia, his journeys most frequently "cling to the roads of the coastal region or to the mariners' routes, even twice or thrice covering for long distances the same track. In the main the apostle's world is to be sought where the sea breeze blows. The coast world of Cilicia, Syria, Palestine, Cyprus, western Asia Minor, Macedonia, Achaia, and

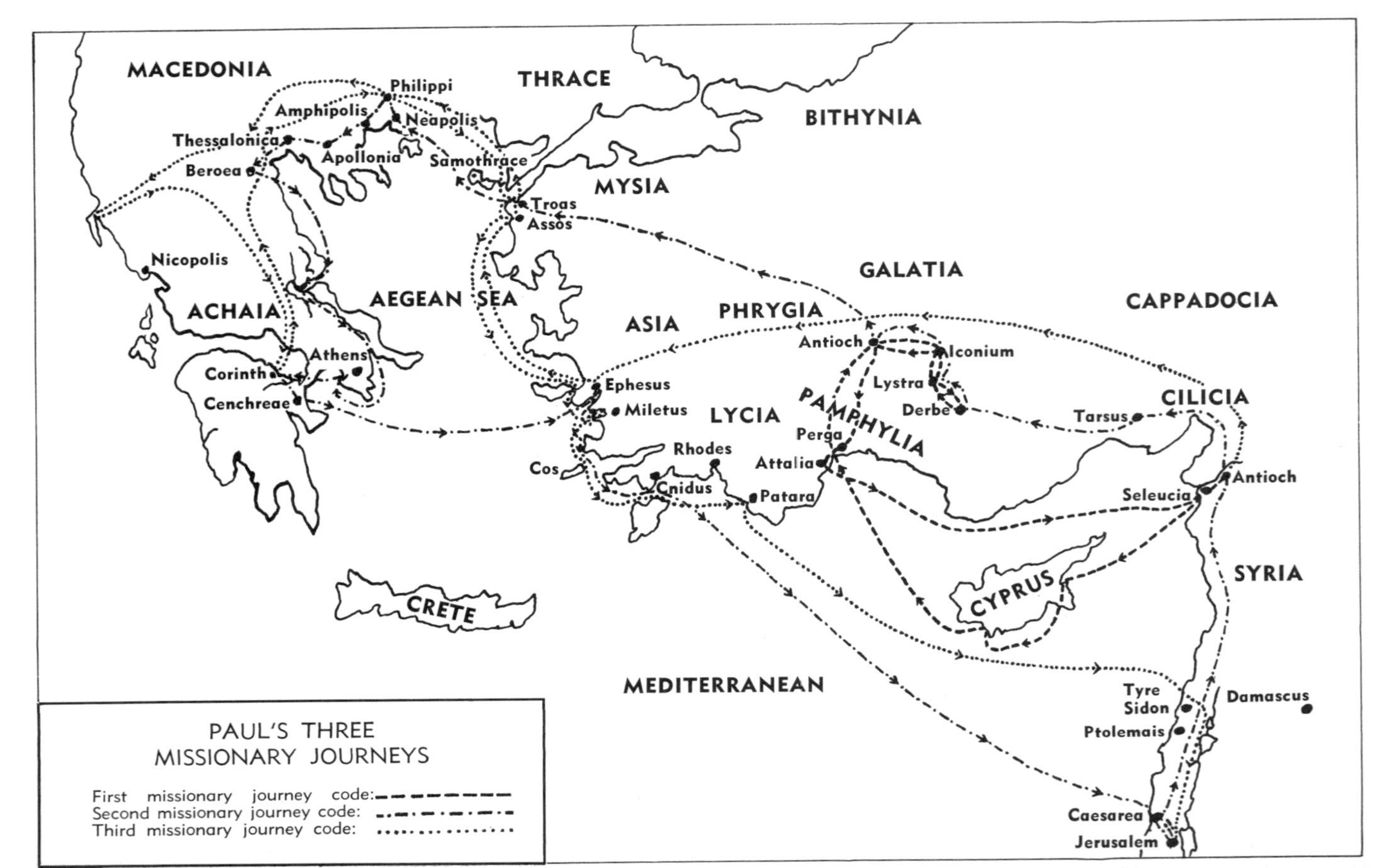
MACEDONIA
THRACE
BITHYNIA
Philippi
Amphipolis
Neapolis
Thessalonica
Apollonia
Samothrace
Beroea
MYSIA
Troas
Assos
Nicopolis
GALATIA
ACHAIA
AEGEAN SEA
CAPPADOCIA
ASIA
PHRYGIA
Antioch
Iconium
Athens
Corinth
Ephesus
Lystra
Cenchreae
Miletus
LYCIA
PAMPHYLIA
Derbe
CILICIA
Tarsus
Perga
Rhodes
Attalia
Cos
Antioch
Cnidus
Patara
Seleucia
SYRIA
CYPRUS
CRETE
MEDITERRANEAN
Tyre
Sidon
Damascus
Ptolemais
Caesarea
Jerusalem
PAUL'S THREE
MISSIONARY JOURNEYS
First missionary journey code:
Second missionary journey code:
Third missionary journey code:

beyond these that of the further west, that is Paul's world.

"The heart of this Pauline world is, however, undoubtedly the wonderful region which may be called 'Aegean': The circle, Ephesus—Troas—Philippi—Thessalonica—Corinth—Ephesus, saw the greatest work of Paul. The New Testament reflects this fact quite clearly in that all the Pauline letters which have been rescued for the canon were either destined for this Aegean circle, or were written within its confines."[3]

To borrow an expression from Adolf Deissmann, "The world of Paul [is] the world of the olive tree!"[4] Paul himself in Romans 11:17 "compares the Gentile world to a wild olive tree. . . . The olive is the living symbol of the unity of the Mediterranean world, it is the tree also of the Bible, both of Old and New Testament. In the names *Mount of Olives* and *Gethsemane* (that is, *oil press)*, as also in the title and name *Messiah, Christ (the Anointed)*, the olive tree has influenced the deepest thoughts and the most holy words of our sacred tradition."[5]

The territory of the olive tree in the Mediterranean region is also "a map of the Jewish or primitive Christian dispersion. As a matter of fact, the zone of the olive tree and the region covered by the Jewish dispersion under imperial Rome are almost exactly coincident. . . . But the olive-tree zone almost exactly coincides also with the map of Paul's missionary journeys, if we leave out Tunis, Algeria, and Morocco; the almost entire lack of olive trees in Egypt is remarkable, and there, too, we have no trace of Paul having traveled. Almost all the important place names in the history of Paul are to be found in the zone of the olive tree: Tarsus, Jerusalem, Damascus, Antioch, Cyprus, Ephesus, Philippi, Thessalonica, Athens, Corinth, Illyricum, Rome (Spain). This world of Paul is relatively uniform, in the first place, in its climatic and other outward conditions of civilization."[6]

Traveling in the region of the olive tree, Paul had few needs. Deissmann says that "without the provision of olives, moreover, Paul's journeys would be inconceivable; the fruit of the olive tree will have played the same role on his sea voyages that it does today on the Levantine steamers and sailing vessels, especially for the sailors and deck passengers. A handful of olives, a piece of bread, and a drink of water—the Levantine traveler requires no more than that!"[7]

In his evangelism along the trade routes of the empire it was relatively easy for Paul to be a Jew to the Jews and a Hellenist of the Hellenists. He had grown up in a Jewish home in Tarsus, where Hellenism was supreme. Educated at Jerusalem under the rabbi Gamaliel, he spoke the language of the Jews—Aramaic (Acts 21:40). But in the city of his birth and youthful years, "a classical center of international intercourse," "the tongue and soul of Hellenism had come to him with the air of Tarsus."[8]

On their journey from Perga to Pisidian Antioch, Paul and Barnabas entered the Roman province of Galatia. In Paul's day Galatia stretched all the way from the region of Pisidian Antioch, Iconium, Lystra, and Derbe, the southern boundary coming within fifty miles of the Mediterranean Sea, northeast to within fifty miles of the southern coast of the Black Sea. According to our concept it did not comprise a vast area, since all Asia Minor is only two thirds the size of Texas. Galatia had received its name from the Gauls, who became masters of the Halys River valley in central Asia Minor during the third century B.C. Rome under General Pompey conquered the region in 64 B.C., and in 25 B.C. it became a Roman province. It included districts south of the ethnic Galatian territory.

The population of Roman Galatia was therefore not homogeneous. In the region of Pisidian Antioch, Iconium, Lystra, and Derbe many Jews had settled, attracted by business opportunities and the encouragement of several Seleucid kings. In the northern part of Roman Galatia lived the ethnic Galatians, the descendants of the Gauls, who were largely pagans.

When Paul preached at Antioch, some Jews enthusiastically received his message (Acts 13:14-43). Others, however, bitterly opposed him and drove him and Barnabas out of town (verses 45, 50). But before that happened, Paul and Barnabas for the first time turned their attention to presenting the gospel to the Gentiles (verses 46-48).

Forced from Antioch, Paul and Barnabas followed the instructions Jesus gave to His disciples when He sent them out two by two to preach. They were not to stay in, but to leave, a place where they were not welcome (Mark 6:11). So the missionaries left, traveling some ninety miles southeast to Iconium, today's populous Turkish city of Konya. Threatened with stoning at Iconium, they moved around twenty miles or so southwest to Lystra, founded by Augustus Caesar as a Roman colony about 6 B.C.

At Lystra, Paul healed a man lame from birth. The people watching the miracle started to worship both Paul and Barnabas as gods, even though the disciples tried their best to prevent this (see Acts 14:8-15). However, others from Pisidian Antioch and Iconium soon arrived and turned the populace against the two. Paul's enemies stoned him and thought him dead. But his converts found him alive and sent him on to Derbe.

Derbe was the farthest extension of Paul's First Missionary Tour. He and Barnabas prepared to return to Antioch in Syria. But instead of taking the short route home through the Cilician Gates, the evangelists decided to retrace their steps, visiting their converts and "strengthening the disciples and encouraging them to remain true to the faith" (verse 22). From Attalia (modern Antalya), about twelve miles from Perga, they took ship back to Seleucia and Antioch in Syria.

In their service for God, Paul and Barnabas had as their first interest the advancement of the cause they unfalteringly served. They had passed the point in life where personal safety held a primary concern, having learned, as A. E. Housman says, that "life, to be sure, is nothing much to lose, but young men think it is." The spiritual stability and welfare of their converts came first. When a person reaches the point in life that he can say, "This is my mission to which I am committed; what happens to me is of secondary importance," then he is liberated from fear to full service for God. The person who always plays it safe is probably a hireling rather than a steward. The steward considers himself expendable, while the hireling does not. Paul was a steward of the mysteries of God and a caretaker of His children. Having surrendered himself to something greater than himself, he could view personal losses without anxiety or regret. In his Epistle to the Philippians he said, "I consider everything a loss compared to the surpassing greatness of knowing Christ Jesus my Lord, for whose sake I have lost all things. I consider them rubbish, that I may gain Christ and be found in him" (chap. 3:8, 9). But he would not throw away his life needlessly, as we see when he took steps to protect himself from flogging by Roman soldiers (Acts 22:24-29) and from a Jewish plot to kill him (chap. 23:13-24). He was ready at all times to do what seemed best, right, and necessary for God's cause without regard to his own welfare.

Paul's method of evangelizing is worth noticing. He copied the method of the Roman Empire. The empire planted Roman colonies in newly conquered areas to Romanize the surrounding area. Such colonists never forgot that they were Romans, and they upheld and practiced Roman law and customs. Through their influence and lives they made Roman citizenship desirable. Some of the nationals then also became

Roman citizens, as for instance Paul's father, and the Roman commander at Jerusalem (chap. 22:28). But even the ethnic non-Romans were proud to call themselves Romans and accepted and upheld Roman laws and customs (see chap. 16:20, 21).

As did the Roman Empire for itself, so Paul "colonized" for God. Later on he wrote to the church members at Philippi, "But we are a colony of heaven" (Phil. 3:20, Moffatt). He concentrated on planting in strategic centers, churches that became nuclei for the spread of Christianity. The leadership in the new congregations came from among the local believers. No strangers or foreigners moved in to direct them (Acts 14:23). Possibly the church did not multiply as fast as it might have with experienced, imported leadership, but it grew more solidly. The people and their leaders were one.

---

[1] Charles F. Pfeiffer and Howard F. Vos, *The Wycliffe Historical Geography of Bible Lands* (Chicago: Moody Press, 1967), p. 307. Much of this chapter is based on information gleaned from this book and from Adolf Deissmann, *Paul: A Study in Social and Religious History* (New York: Harper & Row, 1957; first published in 1912).

[2] Pfeiffer and Vos. *op. cit.*, p. 315.

[3] Deissmann, *op. cit.*, p. 37.

[4] *Ibid.*, p. 38.

[5] *Ibid.*, pp. 38, 39.

[6] *Ibid.*, pp. 39, 40.

[7] *Ibid.*, p. 39.

[8] *Ibid.*, pp. 34, 41.

Galatian Freedom in the Gospel

Jesus Himself confronted Saul on his journey to Damascus to imprison the followers of Jesus. In a vision He said to the blinded persecutor, "'"I have appeared to you to appoint you as a servant and as a witness of what you have seen of me and what I will show you. I will rescue you from your own people and from the Gentiles. I am sending you to open their eyes and turn them from darkness to light, and from the power of Satan to God"'" (Acts 26:16-18). Paul was God's own "'chosen instrument'" (chap. 9:15).

God's chosen witness to the Gentiles was born at Tarsus in Cilicia. Tarsus hugged both sides of the Cydnus River about twelve miles from the Mediterranean Sea and only eighty feet above sea level. The river was navigable, and smaller craft could continue all the way to the city center. The Egyptian queen Cleopatra in 41 B.C. came in her galley to Tarsus for her meeting with Antony.

The trade route coming from the Euphrates over the Amanus Pass and that from Syrian Antioch via the Syrian Gates met about fifty miles east of the city and entered Tarsus as a single road. Then it swung north from Tarsus at a steep climb and passed through the Cilician Gates about thirty miles north of the city.

During the first century A.D. Tarsus was one of the great cities of Asia Minor, with a population, as one writer suggests, of half a million.[1] It was the ancient equivalent of a modern university town with "a seat of Greek higher education."[2] Only the universities of Athens and Alexandria outranked its school of philosophy. The meeting place of the East and the West, where Semite met Hellene, Tarsus was, as Paul stated, "no mean city" (chap. 21:39, K.J.V.).

Paul's parents were Jews of the tribe of Benjamin (Phil. 3:5), but his father was also a Roman citizen (Acts 22:28). The city's timocratic constitution enabled its people to purchase Roman citizenship rights.

Since they belonged to the tribe of Benjamin, his parents bestowed on their son the name of the most renowned man of their tribe—Saul, the first king in Israel. But living in a city with strong Western influences, the parents apparently Grecianized it into a second name—Paul. Probably he used his Jewish name, Saul, when among Jews. Thus Acts 13, which records the beginning of his evangelism among the Gentiles, and onward calls him Paul.

Saul most likely attended a synagogue school in Tarsus. For his university training he went to Jerusalem to sit at the feet of Gamaliel, the foremost Jewish rabbi of the time, rather than enroll in the Hellenistic university of his hometown. Although a Jew, Saul imbibed Greek culture in Tarsus and acquired Greek, or Western, habits of logical reasoning.

"In Paul were integrated those cultural forces which made modern Europe. He was a Hebrew, trained under the great Rabbi Gamaliel. He could talk like a Greek and quote his native Cilician Stoics before the intellectuals of Athens. He could write in muscular Greek his splendid closely argued letters. He was by birth a citizen of Rome.

Only at Tarsus could one so privileged and equipped perfectly emerge. Set at a confluence of East and West, Tarsus produced in balanced form an amalgamated culture. A group of Tarsian Jews had held the coveted citizenship for over a century. Paul could not help seeing the hand of destiny in the circumstances of his birth and education."[3] "The apostle to the Gentiles had to be a Jew, a Greek of Tarsus, and a Roman."[4]

Despite being reared in such a cosmopolitan city, Saul had a strict Jewish family background and rabbinical education and became a dyed-in-the-wool Jew. His father probably was a Pharisee (Acts 26:5). Saul's home and synagogue training together with his studies in Jerusalem under Gamaliel conditioned him also to become, like his father, a Pharisee (Phil. 3:5). Even after "the striking evidences of God's presence with the martyr" Stephen had troubled his conscience, "his education and prejudices, his respect for his former teachers, and his pride of popularity braced him to rebel against the voice of conscience and the grace of God."[5] As a result he became even more fervently devoted to his ancestral religion and adamantly opposed what to him was the rising heresy called the Way (Acts 9:2; 24:14, 22). Being an activist by nature and temperament, rather than a recluse given primarily to contemplation, he determined to do all he could to root out Christianity. He " 'persecuted the followers of this Way to their death' " (chap. 22:4), firmly convinced he was faultless in his "legalistic righteousness" (Phil. 3:6).

Surely Saul with all devout Jews looked for the coming Messiah. But to them the lowly Nazarene Jesus could not possible be He. The Scriptures themselves, they believed, demanded their rejection of His alleged Messiahship. They misapplied the prophecies pertaining to His second coming as the King of glory, believing them to refer to His first advent. The true Messiah, according to their reasoning, was to be a powerful ruler who would free the Jewish people from their Roman oppressors. Both Saul's childhood upbringing and his rabbinical education preconditioned him to join the leaders of his nation in spurning Jesus as the Messiah.

In seeking to bring about the conversion of an individual, God weights His grace so as to counterbalance the particular force of resistance within him. If God did not, many a person would have no real option. His childhood training and education, as in Saul's case, would conclusively rule out his conversion. On the other hand, if we who have been reared in Christian homes and educated in Christian schools would have a Damascus road experience, it would actually deprive us of free choice by overwhelming us in favor of accepting Jesus as our Saviour. Therefore, God does not give us such an encounter. He does what is right for everyone, while protecting each person's free choice.

A father playing on a seesaw, or a teeter-totter, with his small son or daughter sits closer to the fulcrum to balance his child's lesser weight. To move as far away from the fulcrum as his child would prevent any teeter-tottering at all. God deals with people in the same way. He adjusts His weight of evidence for each person so as to give the individual an opportunity to exercise his free choice. Paul refers to the divine principle by saying that "where sin abounded grace superabounded" (Rom. 5:20), Barclay.

Probably Paul never met Jesus during His lifetime on earth, but on the way to Damascus the Saviour confronted him. Then Paul both saw and talked to Jesus (1 Cor. 15:8; Acts 9:3-6); it was an encounter that never faded from his awareness. "Upon the soul of the stricken Jew the image of the Saviour's countenance was imprinted forever."[6] In later years he referred to this experience on several occasions (chaps. 22:5-10; 26:12-18; 1 Cor. 9:1; 15:8).

The theophany humbled the haughty persecutor, but

it also gave him confidence that God had forgiven him for his sins and fully accepted him, both as His child and as an apostle. His meeting with Jesus was a source of constant satisfaction and joy. Ever after, Paul gloried in his possession of a Heaven-sent gospel. With confidence he wrote to the Galatians, "I did not receive it from any man, nor was I taught it; rather, I received it by revelation from Jesus Christ" (Gal. 1:12).

Having experienced that the gospel "is the power of God for the salvation of everyone who believes" (Rom. 1:16), Paul caught fire for God. To him it meant, from that moment on, freedom from sin, guilt, and condemnation, with full and unreserved acceptance by Jesus Christ. His life personally authenticated the gospel.

Jonah in his day was instrumental in saving one of the great cities of the ancient world from destruction. Saved by God from drowning in a raging sea, Jonah convincingly proclaimed God's message to Nineveh. At his preaching "the Ninevites believed God" (Jonah 3:5). And because they believed and repented of their sins, God "had compassion and did not bring upon them the destruction he had threatened" (verse 10).

It is said that after Dante had been through years of exile and solitary wanderings and had at last finished his *Divine Comedy*, the trembling people of Ravenna whispered to one another as he staggered through their streets, "Come and see a man who has just come up out of hell." A person converted by the grace and power of Jesus Christ has indeed come back from a sure road to hell. Paul had experienced a miracle of divine grace. When he preached the saving gospel of Jesus Christ in the fervor of his own experience, many in Galatia accepted it joyously.

Paul's message was Christ-centered. The Damascus road experience had shifted his focus away from the law—by which he had measured himself as a Pharisee (Phil. 3:5, 6)—to Jesus Christ. He had learned that salvation could come to him only by Christ's dying for his sins. Clearly Paul portrayed Jesus to the Galatians "as crucified" (Gal. 3:1)—or He who is the Crucified One (cf. 1 Cor. 1:23; 2:2)—for their sins, but now living.

The apostle firmly believed and accepted Christ's words that " 'I, when I am lifted up from the earth, will draw all men to myself' " (John 12:32). To him, the death on the cross and the resurrection were inseparably united. Whenever speaking about the crucifixion of Jesus, Paul used a grammatical construction (with one exception in 2 Corinthians 13:4) indicating that the cross is not a single incident of the past, but a reality whose influence reaches into the present. But if we could separate Christ's death and resurrection in Paul's thinking, then the resurrection of the living Christ takes precedence, for without it the cross would be but a stumbling block (1 Cor. 15:17). The cross was so prominent in his preaching, however, that Ellen White writes that "always he kept before them [the Gentiles] the cross of Calvary."[7]

So coming to the Galatians, "Paul and his fellow workers proclaimed the doctrine of righteousness by faith in the atoning sacrifice of Christ. They presented Christ as the one who, seeing the helpless condition of the fallen race, came to redeem men and women by living a life of obedience to God's law and by paying the penalty of disobedience. And in the light of the cross many who had never before known of the true God began to comprehend the greatness of the Father's love. Thus the Galatians were taught the fundamental truths concerning 'God the Father' and 'our Lord Jesus Christ, who gave himself for our sins, that he might deliver us from this present evil world, according to the will of God and our Father.' "[8]

"To Paul the cross was the one object of supreme interest. Ever since he had been arrested in his career of persecution against the followers of the crucified

Nazarene he had never ceased to glory in the cross."[9] He keenly realized that the cross is the supreme revelation of God's love and that salvation pivots on it. Paul knew, as P. T. Forsyth stated, that "Christ is to us just what His cross is." Then Forsyth added, "You do not understand Christ till you understand His cross."[10] Paul understood Christ.

"Christ's death proves God's great love for man. It is our pledge of salvation. To remove the cross from the Christian would be like blotting out the sun from the sky. The cross brings us near to God, reconciling us to Him. With the unrelenting compassion of a father's love, Jehovah looks upon the suffering that His Son endured in order to save the race from eternal death, and accepts us in the Beloved.

"Without the cross, man could have no union with the Father. On it depends our every hope. From it shines the light of the Saviour's love, and when at the foot of the cross the sinner looks up to the One who died to save him, he may rejoice with fullness of joy, for his sins are pardoned. Kneeling in faith at the cross, he has reached the highest place to which man can attain.

"Through the cross we learn that the heavenly Father loves us with a love that is infinite. Can we wonder that Paul exclaimed, 'God forbid that I should glory, save in the cross of our Lord Jesus Christ'? Galatians 6:14. It is our privilege also to glory in the cross, our privilege to give ourselves wholly to Him who gave Himself for us. Then, with the light that streams from Calvary shining in our faces, we may go forth to reveal this light to those in darkness."[11]

"Paul's object was to preach the righteousness that comes by faith in Jesus Christ. He took the position that every soul must have a genuine experience in this righteousness. The burning zeal in the heart of Paul compelled him to give the message. He gave assurance of his own faith in the message he bore, and the Holy Spirit accompanied his words with convincing power."[12]

Although the Galatians were idol worshipers, "as the apostles preached to them, they rejoiced in the message that promised freedom from the thralldom of sin. Paul and his fellow workers proclaimed the doctrine of righteousness by faith in the atoning sacrifice of Christ. They presented Christ as the One who, seeing the helpless condition of the fallen race, came to redeem men and women by living a life of obedience to God's law and by paying the penalty of disobedience. And in the light of the cross many who had never before known of the true God, began to comprehend the greatness of the Father's love."[13]

The Galatians responded to Christ's offer " 'to free captives from prison and to release from the dungeon those who sit in darkness' " (Isa. 42:7). Paul perpetuated Christ's earthly ministry " 'to proclaim freedom for the prisoners and recovery of sight for the blind, to release the oppressed' " (Luke 4:18).

Though steeped in darkness of sin, "by hearing with faith" (Gal. 3:2, N.A.S.B.), the Galatians received the Holy Spirit and became "the children of God by faith in Christ" (verse 26, K.J.V.). More than mere nominal members, they became true sons and daughters of God by the infilling of the Spirit, for "if anyone does not have the Spirit of Christ, he does not belong to Christ" (Rom. 8:9). God had indeed sealed them as His own by the gift of the Spirit. The Spirit was the irrefutable sign that the former idol worshipers were now sons and daughters of God. And so Paul in his Epistle reminded them, "Because you are sons, God sent the Spirit of his Son into our hearts, the Spirit who calls out, '*Abba*, Father' " (Gal. 4:6).

---

[1] E. M. Blaiklock, *Cities of the New Testament* (Westwood, N.J.: Fleming H. Revell Company, 1965), p. 19.

[2] Adolf Deissmann, *Paul: A Study in Social and Religious History*, p. 48.

[3] Blaiklock, *op. cit.*, pp. 18, 19.

[4] *Ibid.*, p. 18.
[5] Ellen G. White, *The Acts of the Apostles*, pp. 112, 113.
[6] *Ibid.*, p 115.
[7] *Ibid.*, p. 208.
[8] *Ibid.*, pp. 207, 208.
[9] *Ibid.*, p. 245.
[10] Peter T. Forsyth, *The Cruciality of the Cross* (Grand Rapids, Mich.: Eerdmans, 1966), p. 26.
[11] White, *op. cit.*, pp. 209, 210.
[12] Ellen G. White manuscript 43, March 12, 1907.
[13] White, *The Acts of the Apostles*, pp. 207, 208.

Confrontation

The first Christians were all Jews, as were Jesus and His disciples. They practiced circumcision and observed other Mosaic ordinances. As long as all the members of the church were Jews, it caused no problem. But soon non-Jews entered the church. Peter admitted the Roman centurion Cornelius and his household into the fellowship without their being circumcised and becoming Jews (Acts 10:30-48). Then Greeks joined the church at Antioch in Syria (chap. 11:20, 21).

The church at Antioch grew and soon attracted public attention. The Antiochians possessed great facility in finding and giving people nicknames. The early followers of Christ they may have contemptuously called Christians (verse 26)—"those Christ folk." What their enemies applied to them as a badge of dishonor, the early followers of Jesus transformed into a name of honor. The movement the early Christians developed they themselves called "the Way" (chap. 9:2; 19:9, 23; 24:14, 22).

On their First Missionary Journey, Paul and Barnabas also brought Gentiles into the church. At Paphos on Cyprus the proconsul, Sergius Paulus, believed (chap.

13:6-12). Gentiles became Christians at Pisidian Antioch (verse 48), and the same thing happened at Iconium (chap. 14:1).

By the end of Paul's First Missionary Journey the young Christian church had at least four kinds of members: (1) Aramaic-speaking Jews, who lived largely in Palestine; (2) Hellenistic Jews, or Jews scattered throughout the Roman Empire (some of them were probably also familiar with Aramaic; Paul's family in Tarsus belonged to this group); (3) Jewish proselytes, or non-Jews converted to Judaism and then to the Christian faith (chap. 13:43); (4) Gentiles converted directly to Christianity, like the centurion Cornelius, the proconsul Sergius Paulus, and others won to Christ both at Syrian Antioch and places visited by Paul and his party on the First Missionary Journey.

When the gospel net caught and brought Gentiles into the church, it instantly had to deal with the question of whether they must first become Jews and observe the Jewish rites in order to be true followers of Jesus. The problem initially became acute at Antioch in Syria. Gentiles had joined the Antiochian church in large numbers. Then "some men came down from Judea to Antioch and were teaching the brothers: 'Unless you are circumcised according to the custom taught by Moses, you cannot be saved'" (chap. 15:1).

Circumcision was important to the Jews during the time of Jesus and the early Christian church. Both John the Baptist (Luke 1:59, 60) and Jesus (chap. 2:21) were circumcised. Paul gloried in the personal fulfillment of the rite (Phil. 3:4, 5). Concerning the time of Jesus, Geikie wrote in the 1880s: "Rabbinism was then in its full glory. The strong hand of Herod the Great had suppressed all political agitation for more than a generation, with the result of turning the attention of the rabbis supremely to religious questions, which alone were left for their discussion. The ten thousand legal definitions and decisions, which are now comprised in Jewish religious jurisprudence, were for the most part elaborated in those years, and every devout Israelite made it the labor of his life to observe them faithfully, as far as possible."[1]

No Jewish family would neglect the rite of circumcision. But to be circumcised, the family had to belong to the synagogue. The Jews therefore dreaded to be put out of the synagogue (John 9:22), for "during this time no child could be circumcised nor dead be lamented in the offender's home."[2]

The Jews prided themselves in being the descendants of Abraham (chap. 8:33), and it was from him they had received the rite of circumcision. God Himself originally gave it to the patriarch when he was 99 years old and Ishmael 13, at the time Abraham received the promise of Isaac by Sarah (Gen. 17:10-19, 24, 25). It was a sign of the trust and confidence Abaraham had in God (Rom. 4:11) and of their continuing covenant relationship. All his male descendants would observe it as a constant reminder of God's covenant with them. Non-Jews who wanted to join Israel had to submit to the rite of circumcision (Gen. 34:14-17; Ex. 12:48). In New Testament times the Jews called them proselytes.

For Abraham circumcision had been a sign of his personal friendship relationship with God. But among the Israelites at large it soon lost that meaning. A Jewish family had the rite of circumcision administered to a male child on its eighth day. Males born into Israel consequently had no choice about the rite. They were circumcised because of their parents' decision, not their own. Circumcision therefore did not necessarily denote an Israelite's personal submission to God's will and his faith relationship to Him. It became a tribal sign rather than a personal symbol of faith and trust, as it had been for Abraham.

By Jeremiah's day God could declare that " 'even the

whole house of Israel is uncircumcised in heart' " (Jer. 9:26). The Israelites were no different from surrounding nations, such as Egypt, Edom, Ammon, and Moab. The descendants of Abraham did not listen to God as he did, because "their ears are uncircumcised" (chap. 6:10, Jerusalem). Still the Jews considered the rite as vital. To them—even in the time of the apostles—it signified that they were God's chosen people.

Possibly we as Christians are not too far from the Jews in our thinking. As a young minister I once had an 80-year-old man request that I baptize him into our church. Visiting with him, I soon discovered that he had no concept of what a faith-relationship to Jesus involves. Finally I asked him why he wanted to be baptized. "I am old and sickly and I know that I shall soon die," he said. "But before that, I want to become a member of your church." Ellen G. White wrote that "joining the church is one thing, and connecting with Christ is quite another. Not all the names registered in the church books are registered in the Lamb's book of life. Many, though apparently sincere believers, do not keep up a living connection with Christ. They have enlisted, they have entered their names on the register; but the inner work of grace is not wrought in the heart."[3]

The Judaizers among the Christians continued to insist on circumcision for salvation. In a sense it symbolized all the other ceremonial rituals that the Jews followed. This brought confrontation.

Some of the ceremonial regulations, as for instance a mother's purification after childbirth (Leviticus 12) and a Nazarite's vow (Num. 6:1-21), would cause no particular harm if one chose to observe them. Even Paul himself had no personal aversion against performing some of the Jewish rites. To him, their observance or nonobservance fell into the area of each Christian's free choice. If their observance would further the gospel, he would comply with them; but if they would hinder it, he would ignore them. He expressed his Christian philosophy well in 1 Corinthians 9:19-23, where he says: "Though I am free and belong to no man, I make myself a slave to everyone, to win as many as possible. To the Jews I became like a Jew, to win the Jews. To those under the law I became like one under the law (though I myself am not under the law), so as to win those under the law. To those not having the law I became like one not having the law (though I am not free from God's law but am under Christ's law), so as to win those not having the law. To the weak I became weak, to win the weak. I have become all things to all men so that by all possible means I might save some. I do all this for the sake of the gospel, that I may share in its blessings."

On his last trip to Jerusalem Paul was following or ended a vow at Cenchrea (Acts 18:18), the eastern port of Corinth. And at the urging of James, the leader of the Jerusalem church, and other leading brethren, Paul joined four Nazarites in purification rites (chap. 21:18, 20-24). Neither Paul nor James were Judaizers. To the Judaizers, though, such rites were necessary for salvation.

Paul wanted to please and cooperate with the leadership of the church. Motivated by a "great desire to be in harmony with his brethren" and by "his reverence for the apostles who had been with Christ, and for James, the brother of the Lord, and his purpose to become all things to all men so far as he could without sacrificing principle,"[4] he decided to follow their advice and join the four Nazarites. The leaders wanted him to do this so that " 'everybody will know there is no truth in these reports [that he did not teach and observe the Mosaic law] about you, but that you yourself are living in obedience to the law' " (verse 24). He was influenced by what we today call groupthink. But in trying to please them Paul went too far. He gave the false impression that he both taught and practiced the observance of the

Mosaic law—which, of course, he did not. Ellen G. White comments, "The Spirit of God did not prompt this instruction; it was the fruit of cowardice." Paul "was not authorized of God to concede as much as they asked." But "he was constrained to deviate from the firm, decided course that he had hitherto followed."[5] Groupthink made him deviate from God's plan for him.

Paul fell into the same trap Peter had fallen into at Syrian Antioch. There Peter submitted to groupthink in order to please his fellow believers who had come from Jerusalem. Consequently Peter ceased to eat with the Gentile converts in order to please the Christian Jews (Gal. 2:11-14). Now Paul, who had publicly rebuked Peter for his departure from God's plan at that time, made the same mistake to satisfy the same faction.

Paul and Barnabas, the missionaries to the Gentiles, objected to circumcision as a prerequisite for salvation. They saw no need for Gentile converts to first become Jews in order to become Christians. In order to settle the issue, "Paul and Barnanbas were appointed, along with some other believers, to go up to Jerusalem to see the apostles and elders about this question" (Acts 15:2).

Although Paul had received his apostleship directly from Heaven, he still looked to the leaders of the church for direction and guidance. He had not begun his missionary work until those at Antioch, prompted by the Holy Spirit, asked him to do so (chap. 13:2, 3), which was at least fourteen years after he himself had experienced his personal call to evangelism on the road to Damascus. And even though he and Barnabas were fully convinced under the guidance of the Holy Spirit that the Gentile Christians were not to observe the Mosaic law, they did not single-handedly decide the question. Instead they submitted it to the leaders of the whole church at the Jerusalem Council.

"To neglect or despise those whom God has appointed to bear the responsibilities of leaderhip in connection with the advancement of the truth, is to reject the means that He has ordained for the help, encouragement, and strength of His people. For any worker in the Lord's cause to pass these by, and to think that his light must come through no other channel than directly from God, is to place himself in a position where he is liable to be deceived by the enemy and overthrown."[6]

Titus, a Gentile convert, accompanied Paul and Barnabas as a member of the delegation from Antioch (Gal. 2:1, 3). At the council Peter mentioned how he had allowed Gentile Christians into fellowship. He had done so because God had obviously accepted them as He had the Jewish Christians, "'by giving the Holy Spirit to them, just as he did to us'" (Acts 15:8). James, the leader of the Jewish believers, summed up the council discussion by saying: "'Brothers, listen to me. Simon has described to us how God at first showed his concern by taking from the Gentiles a people for himself. . . . It is my judgment, therefore, that we should not make it difficult for the Gentiles who are turning to God. Instead we should write to them, telling them to abstain from food polluted by idols, from sexual immorality, from the meat of strangled animals and from blood'" (verses 13-20).

The sentiment Peter and James expressed went contrary to the wishes of the Judaizers. "They were slow to discern that all the sacrificial offerings had but prefigured the death of the Son of God, in which type met antitype, and after which the rites and ceremonies of the Mosaic dispensation were no longer binding."[7] The Judaizers had accepted the Christian faith but had been unable to shed their ceremonial Jewish heritage.

The council's decision agreed with the views of Peter and James. It was not merely their opinion, but "it seemed good to the Holy Spirit" (verse 28).

As mentioned previously, Titus attended the council. Probably Paul had brought him along specifically to test the validity of his position that Gentile Christians need not be circumcised. Apparently some Christian believers maintained even at the council that he ought to be circumcised. But Paul stood his ground, supported by Peter, James, and the council action, so that "not even Titus, who was with me, was compelled to be circumcised, even though he was a Greek," the apostle wrote in Galatians 2:3.

Titus is possibly the most important person Paul mentions in his Epistle to the Galatians. He became the test case of the position the leaders had just reached at Jerusalem. His uncircumcision was and remained Paul's best weapon for the defense of the pure gospel against the assaults of the Judaizers, who insisted on circumcision as a prerequisite for becoming a Christian. The apostle could later refer to the unanimous decision of the leadership of the whole Christian church to let Titus remain uncircumcised despite the urging of the Judaizers at the Jerusalem Council.

Paul and the apostles did not reject circumcision as something sinful to retain and practice, but the council made it clear that it was not necessary for justification or salvation. Out of respect toward the Jewish Christians, and possibly out of charity toward those weak in faith, however, the Jewish Christians were free to observe it, and to comply also with other features of the ceremonial law until they had time to adjust their thinking. No one was to be forced to be circumcised in order to become a Christian, but neither was anyone to be prevented from being circumcised if he chose it. The Christian leaders wanted all to know that circumcision was not necessary for justification or salvation, but that it was a permissible option.

The Jerusalem Council devoted no thought or discussion to releasing the Gentile Christians from observing the moral law, however. They discussed circumcision "after the manner of Moses" (Acts 15:1,

K.J.V.) and "the law of Moses" (verse 5, K.J.V.). But the moral law, the transcript of God's character delineated in the commandments that God Himself spoke and wrote on tables of stone at Sinai, was not an issue. Paul and the Judaizers never had any arguments over the obervance of the moral law by Gentile Christians. The Council of Jerusalem sought solely to determine the relationship of the Gentile Christians to the Mosaic law.

Under ordinary circumstances the leaders of the Jerusalem church might have permitted Titus to be circumcised if he himself had chosen it. But when the Judaizers urged his circumcision, the church leaders then said No. To have compelled him to be circumcised would have negated the Jerusalem Council.

In a unanimous decision, or "with one accord" (verse 25, K.J.V.), the council decided not to impose the Mosaic ordinances on the Gentile converts. But unfortunately the Jerusalem session did not end the agitation for the Gentiles to observe the Mosaic law. The problem became especially acute among the churches of Galatia. To allay the controversy and restore peace among the Galatian believers, Paul wrote his Epistle to the Galatians. It presented the Christian understanding of the gospel, of faith in Jesus as the basis for justification and salvation. Later and in more detail he discussed the same issue in his Epistle to the Romans.

The Jerusalem Council testified to the fact that Christianity had jumped the bounds of Judaism. The old "bottles" were being broken: Christianity was entering new paths both geographically, racially, and religiously. It was freeing itself from Jewish limitations. Paul—who believed and taught that "neither circumcision nor uncircumcision means anything; what counts is a new creation" (Gal. 6:15)—was the driving force.

The apostle wanted to free all followers of Christ from the erroneous concept that they could save themselves by observing the Mosaic law. "Galatians is Paul's declaration of religious independence from men and dependence on God. It is the Magna Charta of the Christian faith, repudiating all authorities, institutions, customs, and laws that interfere with the direct access of the individual to his God."[8] But he goes beyond circumcision and its corollaries and teaches that we cannot obtain salvation through any law—not even the ten-commandment law. It is impossible to merit anything by a law already violated or broken.

What God was—and is—interested in is not circumcision of the flesh, but of the heart. It means joyful willingness to heed His will and go His way rather than rebelliously insisting on one's own will and way. "A man is not a Jew if he is only one outwardly, nor is circumcision merely outward and physical. No, a man is a Jew if he is one inwardly; and circumcision is circumcision of the heart, by the Spirit (Rom. 2:28, 29).

"**Circumcision of Christ.** That is, the circumcision that Christ performs, not that performed on Him. True spiritual circumcision, the removal and burying of the evil tendencies of the heart, is brought about through the agency of Jesus Christ Himself. His power alone can remove the old life and create a new man. From the ceremony of circumcision Paul draws a spiritual lesson for the Christian."[9]

As God gave the Israelites circumcision, so He has provided us with the Sabbath as a sign (Eze. 20:20) of our intimate friendship with Him. Is it possible that some of us, like the ancient Israelites, may have the sign without the relationship with God that the Sabbath should indicate? That makes us foreigners to God. "'"No foreigner uncircumcised in heart and flesh is to enter my sanctuary"'" (chap. 44:9). We represent God; His reputation rests in our hands. What do people think about Him from our depiction of Him?

Hopefully our witness for Him is better than that of the Jews in Jeremiah's day; they were no different from the surrounding nations. And they gloried in being physical descendants of Abraham. But to be saved, we too must be descendants of Abraham—descendants in faith. "If you belong to Christ, then you are Abraham's seed, and heirs according to the promise" (Gal. 3:29). And "a man is a Jew if he is one inwardly; and circumcision is circumcision of the heart, by the Spirit, not by the written code. Such a man's praise is not from men, but from God" (Rom. 2:29).

---

[1] Cunningham Geikie, *The Life and Words of Christ*, Vol. I, p. 176.
[2] Ellen G. White, *The Desire of Ages*, p. 472.
[3] ———, *Testimonies*, vol. 5, p. 278.
[4] ———, *The Acts of the Apostles*, p. 405.
[5] *Ibid.*, pp. 404, 405.
[6] *Ibid.*, p. 164.
[7] *Ibid.*, p. 189.
[8] From Raymond T. Stamm, in *The Interpreter's Bible*, vol. 10, p. 429. Used by permission of Abingdon Press.
[9] *The SDA Bible Commentary* (Washington, D.C.: Review and Herald Pub. Assn., 1957), vol. 7., p. 203.

Apostasy in Galatia

The Jerusalem Council concluded that Gentile Christians need not submit to circumcision and observe the Mosaic regulations. Its decision applied to all the Christian churches. But not all Jewish converts were satisfied with the outcome. Many disagreed or found fault with it and independently assumed the responsibility to visit churches containing Gentile believers and teach them that in order to be saved they must submit to circumcision and oberve the Mosaic code.

Such Jewish zealots, or Judaizers, dogged Paul's converts and stirred up trouble, particularly in Syria and Galatia. They tried to convince Gentile converts that there was no salvation apart from becoming Jews. Among the Galatians they found a fertile field.

The Judaizers believed themselves to be both born and reared in righteousness—"'Jews by birth and not "Gentile sinners"'" (Gal. 2:15). The Jews regarded as sinners those who did not observe the ceremonial laws, without any reference to morals or ethics—they were simply sinners. But not even the phrase "'Jews by birth'" conveys the full scope of Paul's meaning. "It was not only birth but a nurture, a way of life, a heritage, a destiny, and a missionary task that gave the Jew a *nature* (K.J.V.) different from sinners . . . of Gentile stock. . . . The Jews did not claim to be sinless, but they did claim to be friends and not enemies of the one God, beside whom there was no other, who was just and holy and good, and whose will they were earnestly trying to do. But because Paul took this mission with utter seriousness, he learned from sad experience that the Jews were not good enough, and that salvation by merit for obedience to law was impossible (Rom. 2:1-3:20)."[1]

The Christian Judaizers gloried in their privileged status of being the specially chosen of God. They were the true spiritual kinsmen of the Jews who said to Jesus, "We be Abraham's seed"; "We have one Father, even God" (John 8:33, 41, K.J.V.). Relying on their heritage and on the law for salvation (see Rom. 2:17), they firmly believed that, as in Old Testament times, to become part of God's people, even after the death of Christ, a person must be circumcised (Gen. 34:14-17; Ex. 12:48). Thus they infiltrated among the Galatians "to spy on the freedom" (Gal. 2:4) the Galatians had in Christ.

Being young in the faith, the Galatian believers lost their confidence in Christ. After reconsidering their relationship to Him, they decided that it seemed more reasonable to make themselves acceptable to God through the Jewish rites and rituals. And so they began to try to be justified, or put right with God, by wanting "to be under the law" (chap. 4:21), seeking to be "perfected by the flesh" (chap. 3:3, N.A.S.B.), or by what human effort could accomplish through Jewish rituals and the ceremonial law.

Apart from religious conviction, the early Christians found a political advantage in being circumcised. The authorities regarded those circumcised as Jews, and they enjoyed certain privileges in the Roman Empire. Hence those advocating circumcision "saw in it a passport to safety should persecution arise. Circumcision would keep them safe from the hatred of the Jews and the law of Rome alike."[2]

When Paul discusses justification by faith in Galatians, he refers primarily to the ceremonial, or Mosaic, law. Its symbol was circumcision. However, in a broader sense "the term 'law' in Galatians stands for the entire revelation, at Sinai, of God's rules for His children—moral laws, civil statutes, and ceremonial ritual. To these the Jews later added a ponderous array of man-made laws. They mistakenly thought that by their own strength they could give perfect obedience to these laws, and that by such obedience they could earn their own salvation. Galatians is concerned not so much with any of these laws as such, but with the erroneous idea that a man can earn his own salvation by rigorous adherence to various legal requirements. The issue is one of salvation by faith versus salvation by works."[3] When the Galatian believers relinquished their hope of justification as a free gift from God through faith in Jesus, they substituted the yoke of Jewish legalism for freedom in Christ.

To counteract the confusion the Judaizers caused in Galatia, Paul penned his Epistle to the Galatians, probably from Corinth around A.D. 57 or 58.[4] He begins by defending his apostolate, which the Galatians had questioned. In doing so, he introduces himself in a unique way, stating that he is "an apostle—sent not from men nor by man, but by Jesus Christ and God the Father" (chap. 1:1). None of his other Epistles have an introduction like this. In some he just gives his name (1 Thess. 1:1; 2 Thess. 1:1); in others he calls himself "an apostle of Christ Jesus by the will of God" (Eph. 1:1; Col. 1:1; 2 Tim. 1:1) or "by the command of God" (1 Tim. 1:1); "a servant of God and an apostle of Jesus Christ" (Titus 1:1); the servant "of Christ Jesus" (Phil. 1:1); or "called to be an apostle of Christ Jesus by the will of God" (1 Cor,

1:1). He wanted his letter to have a special authority.

His gospel was not man-made, nor had he obtained it through human instruments. Like the other apostles, Paul had received it directly from Jesus Christ Himself."I did not receive it from any man," he writes, "nor was I taught it; rather, I recieved it by revelation from Jesus Christ" (Gal. 1:12). And he, like the other apostles, had seen the Lord (verses 15, 16; cf. 1 Cor. 9:1)—the Risen One. To refute the erroneous teachings of the Judaizers, "Paul magnifies his office; he will not take a back seat to any other apostle. He boasts that his doctrine and office are from God alone, in order that he might silence the boast of the false apostles."[5]

He expresses no gratefulness to God for their faith and Christian witness, as he did in writing to the churches in Thessalonica, Philippi, Corinth, Colossae, and Rome (1 Thess. 1:2, 3; 2 Thess. 1:3; Phil. 1:3-5; 1 Cor. 1:4, 5; Col. 1:3, 4; Rom. 1:8). Nor does he call the members in Galatia saints (holy ones), as he does the believers in Philippi, Corinth, Ephesus, Colossae, and Rome (Phil. 1:1; 1 Cor. 1:2; Eph. 1:1; Col. 1:2; Rom. 1:7). Rather, he speaks of sorrow at their departure from the gospel he had proclaimed to them. "I am surprised at you! In no time at all you are deserting the one who called you by the grace of Christ" (Gal. 1:6, T.E.V.). The only way Paul could explain their departure from the true faith was that the Galatians had been thrown "into confusion" (chap. 5:10) by being "bewitched" (chap. 3:1).

Fervently he tried to convince his spiritual children that they have made a mistake by forsaking the gospel of salvation by grace through faith in Jesus Christ. Categorically and vehemently he states that their new teachers do not teach a true gospel. If theirs differs from the one he had presented to them, it is a deception from hell. "Even if we or an angel from heaven shall preach a gospel other than the one we preached to you, let him be eternally condemned!" (chap. 1:8).

Paul did not mince words. He "stopped short only of profanity. He could have used no stronger language and have remained within the bounds of propriety. . . . He never lost his balance. He was severe because he so intended. He wrote to the Corinthians out of anguish of heart, through tears, for their failure in Christian living; he was even more severe in his letter to the Galatians, for the very core of the Christian message was at stake. Remembering that the letter to the Galatians has changed history, that all might have been different had Paul written differently, that its 149 verses altered the world, one is not surprised to find him using words that were dynamite. They were God's words before they were Paul's.

"Some advocates of extreme religious tolerance hold that what a man believes is his own business. They insist that life and work, as sure demonstrations of his belief, are the tests that matter, at least as far as the public is concerned; that every man's religion is larger than he can define; that life is more definitive than theology. Keeping brotherly is all that matters, say they. Why quibble? Be practical. Cooperate or unite for worthy service programs in the spirit of Jesus and men will be led into the truth they need to live by. Let the theologians argue, not they. Theologians, as far as they are concerned, are left to split hairs, burn the midnight oil, and live on salaries which to many laymen symbolize their worth. Not so with the drawing of sharp social distinctions. Not so with United States Supreme Court lawyers, who split hairs so sharply that many of the court's most history-making decisions have been by 5-4 votes. Not so with airplane pilots, whose split-second navigation means landing safely or cracking up. Not so with the scientist, whose split-cell research in laboratory or clinic means life or death. And in high and holy fact it is not so with theology either. It is from men like Paul and books like Galatians that contenders for the significance of doctrine get their ammunition. Such men and books sharpen the church's conscience to perform its historic function of being the custodian of truth. Such men cannot understand the morals of, nor will they have fellowship with, those who are tolerant of doctrinal looseness or unconcern; because *what man in his heart believes, soon or late he begins to be and do.*"[6]

Occasionally we think that tolerance is the supreme virtue. But that is not the case. There is a sin of tolerance. With Satan anything goes, but not so with God. With Him there are sacred principles, and also rules emanating from them that we must not violate. For Adam and Eve the principle was obedience, and the rule was Don't eat of the tree of knowledge. Going against it brought disaster.

Next Paul shows the bewildered Galatians—and all Christians—that it is impossible to be justified, or put into right and life-giving relationship with God, through *any* law. " 'By observing the law no one will be justified' " (chap. 2:16), and " 'If righteousness could be gained through the law, Christ died for nothing!' " (verse 21). He becomes even more emphatic by saying that "all who rely on observing the law are under a curse" (chap. 3:10).

A violated law can only condemn. No transgressed law can justify and save. The same thing applies to the Ten Commandments. After we have broken one of them, they only sentence us to death, since the violation of God's law is sin, and "the wages of sin is death" (Rom. 6:23). The consequence is "that the very commandment that was intended to bring life actually brought death" (chap. 7:10). But "Christ redeemed us from the curse of the law by becoming a curse for us" (Gal. 3:13). He was accursed for us when the Roman soldiers nailed Him to Calvary's tree, thus taking away the curse from us. Life and sonship come through faith in Jesus (verse 26; John 1:12).

By attempting to gain acceptance with God and obtain salvation by the performance of the Mosaic law, the Galatians had separated themselves from God. "You have been severed from Christ, you who are seeking to be justified by law; you have fallen from grace" (Gal. 5:4, N.A.S.B.).

In rejecting the gospel of salvation by grace through faith in Jesus Christ, the Galatians had also spurned Paul as their friend and teacher. Initially they had received Paul as an angel, or as "Christ Jesus himself" (chap. 4:14), but now they regarded him as an "enemy" (verse 16).

Many find it difficult to differentiate between ideas, concepts, and teachings, and the person who holds or teaches them. They dislike the person because they disagree with his views. In the same way we are prone to hate the sinner because of our reaction to his sin. As we mature we should learn to separate ideas from the person who holds them. Jesus hates sin, but He loves the sinner. If Christ had been unable to make a distinction between us and what we think and do, then He would not have been willing to die for you and me. Our very salvation depends on His willingness and ability to distinguish between the person and what he does and thinks. But the Galatians were like many of us. When they discarded Paul's teachings regarding the gospel and turned to Judaizing teachers with "a different gospel" (chap. 1:6), they also rejected him as their friend and began to hate him.

But Paul did not let the Galatians' hostility intimidate him or change his attitude toward them. He still loved them and was concerned about their best good and wished he could be with them to help them in their moment of spiritual need (chap. 4:19, 20).

In this respect Paul reflected the character of God, who loves us all irrespective of what we are and do. God is unchanging love and never forgets His own. He tells every one of us, "'I have engraved you upon the palms of my hands'" (Isa. 49:16).

Paul looked upon the straying Galatians as a mother does her children. The very price of suffering she endured in bringing them into the world makes them so much more precious in her sight. As a parent sorrows deeply for a child or children who are in trouble, so anxiety filled Paul for his Galatian "children" (Gal. 4:19). He "pleaded with those who had once known in their lives the power of God, to return to their first love of gospel truth."[7]

It is possible that some of the Galatians had been converted not to Christ, but to Paul. So when he left and new teachers arrived, the people became attached to them. The same danger exists today. A person may become a disciple of a certain preacher or evangelist rather than a follower of God. To many the inner conflict between commitment to truth and attachment to a charismatic teacher becomes indeed wrenching. Consequently we must guard our affections and keep them always subordinated to the will of God. Satan "secures multitudes to himself by attaching them by the silken cords of affection to those who are enemies of the cross of Christ."[8] As loyal Christians, all our attachments, be they parental, filial, conjugal, or social, will remain subordinate to our loyalty to God and His expressed will.

Paul wanted the Galatians and all Christian believers always to remember that their hope of acceptance with God and their salvation rest on His free grace and not on compliance with rules and rituals. To that end he begins his Epistle by reminding them of God's grace (chap. 1:3). He ends his letter by committing them anew to the grace of God (chap. 6:18). In between he tries to disabuse them of any hope of salvation and divine acceptance through circumcision and a return to the rituals of the ceremonial law. Indeed, his aim throughout the entire Epistle is to direct their eyes again to the cross of Jesus as their only source of salvation. Paul knew that "to remove the cross from the Christian would be like blotting the sun from the sky. . . . Without the cross, man could have no union with the Father."[9] This was his burden as he agonizingly wrote his Epistle to his Galatian converts.

"For a time Paul [had] lost his hold on the minds of those who had been deceived; but relying on the word and power of God, and refusing the interpretations of the apostate teachers, he was able to lead the converts to see that they had been deceived, and thus defeat the purposes of Satan. The new converts came back to the faith, prepared to take their position intelligently for the truth."[10]

In achieving this, Paul wielded no vested power or authority over the Galatians. The genius that extended his influence over them was rather, as Deissmann expresses it, "the suggestive power of his entirely trustful and entirely brotherly personality which bound people to him."[11] Through his selfless ministry among them Paul had earned their respect and hence power or authority over them.

Without the Galatian apostasy, Paul would probably never have written an Epistle like Galatians, nor his later letter to the Romans, designed to prevent a similar apostasy in the Roman church. But in His providence God prompted him to compose both. The two Epistles have constantly counterbalanced the ever-present human tendency to trust to activity and human merits for salvation, and have turned the eyes of sinners to God and His love, whom to know "is life eternal" (John 17:3, K.J.V.).

---

[1] From Raymond T. Stamm, in *The Interpreter's Bible*, vol. 10, pp. 482, 483. Used by permission of Abingdon Press.

[2] William Barclay, *The Letters to the Galatians and Ephesians*, revised edition (Philadelphia: The Westminster Press, 1976), p. 56.

[3] *The SDA Bible Commentary*, vol. 6, p. 933.

[4] *Ibid.*, p. 932.

[5] H. T. Lehmann (ed.), *Luther's Works*, vol. 35, p. 384.

[6] From O. F. Blackwelder, in *The Interpreter's Bible*, vol. 10, pp. 450, 451. (Italics supplied.) Used by permission of Abingdon Press.

[7] Ellen G. White, *The Acts of the Apostles*, p. 388.

[8] ———, *The Great Controversy*, p. 597.

[9] ———, *The Acts of the Apostles*, p. 209.

[10] Ellen G. White manuscript 43, 1907.

[11] Adolph Deissmann, *Paul: A Study in Social and Religious History*, p. 249.

Self-righteous Believers

Reading the Epistle of James is not a joyous experience like that of reading Paul's letter to the Philippians or to the Ephesians. Philippians throughout breathes joy, and Ephesians lifts the reader to the very pinnacles of heaven. James's Epistle, on the other hand, contains tacit rebukes from beginning to end. It urges readers to demonstrate their faith by their deeds.

The writer of the Epistle must have been well known to all his readers because he introduces himself simply as "James, a servant of God and of the Lord Jesus Christ" (chap. 1:1). Tradition commonly identifies him as the brother of Jesus (see Mark 6:3).

During Jesus' ministry James and his brothers did not sympathize with Him and would have liked to restrain Him (Matt. 12:46-50; Mark 3:21, 31-35). "For even his own brothers did not believe in him," John stated (John 7:5). Before the crucifixion they did not accept their brother Jesus as the Messiah. The circumstances of their conversion are unknown, but between the resurrection and the ascension Jesus appeared to James (1 Cor. 15:7), and Luke mentions the brothers of Jesus as part of the believers prior to Pentecost (see Acts

1:14). Paul acknowledges James as an apostle (Gal. 1:19).

In the organization of the postresurrection church, James became the leader of the members at Jerusalem. When an angel delivered Peter from prison, the disciple sent a message to James (Acts 12:17). Peter and James met with Paul on his first postconversion visit to Jerusalem (Gal. 1:18, 19). James presided at the Jerusalem Council (Acts 15), and he, Peter, and John, the pillars of the Jerusalem church, gave Paul and Barnabas the right hand of fellowship for their preaching of the gospel to the Gentiles (Gal. 2:9). Paul delivered the collection from the Gentile churches to him (see Acts 21:17-20). The leader of many thousands of Jews (see verse 20) in the church, James addresses his Epistle to Christians in the Dispersion as "the twelve tribes scattered among the nations" (James 1:1).

Many scholars think that the believers he addresses were Jewish Christians. Others disagree. "His [James's] epistle, then, is addressed to the entire church; it cannot be limited or restricted to Jewish believers of the dispersion."[1] As to its time of composition there is "an absence of the issues faced by Paul in Romans 4 and Galatians 3 after the Jerusalem Conference (A.D. 49)." Thus James probably composed his book before the Jerusalem Council, and it "may indeed be the earliest New Testament book."[2]

What James thinks about his readers we may gather from the way he opens his discourse. It lacks a preamble, commonly found in most New Testament Epistles, and contains no thanks to God for them and their faithfulness in Christ, or the virtue they possess and manifest in their service for God. Nor does it include a petition for their needs. Rather, James abruptly begins to stress the necessity of ethical, moral behavior by pointing out what a Christian ought not to do, say, and be. In doing so he sounds almost like an Old Testament prophet and uses frequent imperatives, of which his short book contains more than fifty.

The Jewish Christians to whom James probably directed his Epistle had received and accepted the Christian teaching of salvation by faith in Jesus. As Jews they had most likely been morally reputable members of society, with laudable ethics even before their conversion. They had not been moral derelicts like some of the believers Paul would later gather in his gospel net in the great port city of Corinth (1 Cor. 6:9-11). Consequently no great behavioral changes had occurred in the lives of James's audience. Their impeccable life style had not measurably changed, nor had their acceptance of Christ as their Saviour led to good thoughts and deeds. They were just like the rich young ruler.

James, commonly called the Just, in his corrective Epistle faithfully echoes the ethical teachings of Jesus by giving detailed practical advice regarding the life of a true believer in Him. He "reminds his Jewish Christian readers that the moral law is still binding upon God's people. It must be kept in every point (chap. 2:10-13). Indeed, the new law of Jesus is a 'perfect law' and a 'law of liberty' (chaps. 1:25; 2:12). Above all, Christians must fulfill 'the royal law' (chap. 2:8), the law governing the citizens of God's Kingdom (verse 5), namely: 'Thou shalt love thy neighbour as thyself.' First promulgated through Moses (Lev. 19:18), then sanctioned by Jesus (Mark 12:31), this law is still in force. God is not impressed by our religious knowledge or outward profession. He desires obedience and inward sincerity. It is not enough to hear the word. We must do it."[3]

In James 1:27 he encapsules in one short verse the believer's threefold responsibility to God, to his neighbor, and to himself: "Religion that God our Father accepts as pure and faultless is this: to look after orphans and widows in their distress and to keep oneself from being polluted by the world."

Not being polluted by the world presupposes "self-control," or "temperance" in the King James Version of the Bible (Gal. 5:23). This is God's expressed will for all human beings. The crowning human virtue, it becomes ours as we surrender ourselves fully to God.

Self-control will reveal itself in well-ordered speech. "If anyone appears to be 'religious' but cannot control his tongue, he deceives himself and we may be sure that his religion is useless" (James 1:26, Phillips).

James uses several graphic illustrations to show the vital consequences of our use of the only bundle of muscles in the whole body attached at only one end. He compares it to the rudder of a ship. Although exceedingly small when compared with the ship, the rudder guides the whole vessel (chap. 3:4). The tongue resembles a spark that can cause a blazing forest fire (verse 5) or an unquenchable holocaust. And it reminds him of the small bit in the horse's mouth, which the rider uses to direct and control the animal's movements (verse 3). He goes on to show the inconsistency of both praising God and cursing with the same tongue (verses 9, 10). To James the idea is incongruous and should be as impossible as for a fig tree to bear olives (verse 12) or for the same spring to issue both fresh and salt water (verse 11).

But although it is contradictory for a Christian both to praise and curse with the same tongue, it is all too common. As human beings we enter the world with carnal natures not subject to the will of God. Through the new birth we also become partakers of the divine nature (2 Peter 1:4). A Christian therefore has both a human and a divine nature. Which of the two will rule? That depends on each person's moment-by-moment choices. Jesus, our Saviour and Example, chose to subject His humanness to the divine. "'Father,'" He prayed, "'if you are willing, take this cup from me; yet not my will, but yours be done'" (Luke 22:42). "In Christ there was a *subjection of the human to the divine.* He clothed His divinity with humanity, and placed His own person under obedience to divinity."[4]

As a result of Jesus' willing submission to His Father's guidance, He never spoke unadvisedly and foolishly. To the unbelieving Jews, Jesus declared, "'I have not spoken on my own authority, but the Father who sent me has commanded me what I must say and speak'" (John 12:49, T.E.V.). On another occasion He stated, "'I do nothing on my own authority, but I say only what the Father has instructed me to say'" (chap. 8:28, T.E.V.).

Never did Jesus speak impetuously or unwisely. The leading of His Father through the Spirit enabled Him to speak judiciously at all times and under all circumstances. Even when harassed by the scribes and Pharisees or physically abused at His trial, He did not lose control of what He said.

When we study His life and notice His calm behavior under the most trying circumstances, we might wish we were like Him and could receive such intimate guidance from God. We don't want to react rashly and unwisely to provocation. But to escape our common pitfalls we need to calm ourselves before God. The best way to do so is to study our Bibles devotionally each day. For most of us the preferable time is in the morning. Then during the leisure moments of the day, we can turn our thoughts to Jesus as we recall the words from His Book. Our "only security against rash, ambitious movements is to keep the heart in harmony with Christ."[5] Mrs. White assures us that "those who study the Bible, counsel with God, and rely upon Christ will be enabled to act wisely at all times and under all circumstances."[6]

If we are but willing, God will teach us both what to do and what to say, and how to say it. The promise He gave to Moses is also for you and me: "'I will help you speak and will teach you what to say' " (Ex. 4:12). So we shall be able to talk in a way pleasing to God at all times and under all circumstances, for "angels will be by our side, prompting us to a better course, choosing our words for us, and influencing our actions."[7]

But the tongue is not the root of the trouble. It is just an index of the mind. " 'The things that come out of the mouth come from the heart' " (Matt. 15:18). To the Pharisees, Jesus commented: " 'Make a tree good and its fruit will be good, or make a tree bad and its fruit will be bad, for a tree is recognized by its fruit. You brood of vipers, how can you who are evil say anything good? For out of the overflow of the heart the mouth speaks. The good man brings good things out of the good stored up in him, and the evil man brings evil things out of the evil stored up in him' " (chap. 12:33-35).

Jesus went to the root of the matter. The mouth only voices what fills the heart, or the mind. In the Old Testament, God through the Holy Spirit inspired the wise man to write that as a selfish man "thinks within himself, so is he" (Prov. 23:7, N.A.S.B.). Effective control of speech depends ultimately on a heart and mind under the continuous guidance of the Holy Spirit. "I will take away your stubborn heart of stone and give you an obedient heart" (Eze. 36:26, T.E.V.). The new heart God gives us will store contents in keeping with His will.

The source of both correct speech and action is not rigid self-control, but a God-given new heart, or mind, willingly susceptible to the promptings of the Holy Spirit. Then the tongue will express divinely prompted thoughts and words. "If a person never makes a mistake in what he says, he is perfect," James states (chap. 3:2, T.E.V.). It was indeed true of the man Jesus.

Of all the gifts God has bestowed on man, none is of greater potential good than that of speech.[8] Hopeful words of love may rekindle a spirit of enthusiasm in someone who has almost relinquished his or her hold on life. They can strengthen the bruised reed or revive the smoldering wick (see Matt. 12:20), as did the gracious words Jesus spoke to the woman caught in the act of adultery (John 8:3-11). "Sweet, kind words are as dew and gentle showers to the soul."[9] The right thing said at the right time can give strength for victory over temptation. "Kindly words simply spoken, little attentions simply bestowed, will sweep away the clouds of temptation and doubt that gather over the soul."[10]

On the other hand, lacking the Spirit's fruit of self-control, one's speech may become an instrument of evil. Withering words may kill just as surely as does the cannibal or murderer.

A mind under the constant guidance of God will reveal its Mentor by well-chosen and appropriate words. Such a mind will obviate the problems that James called to the attention of his readers—like partiality for the rich over the poor (chap. 2:1-13), boastful self-assurance (chap. 4:13-16), self-seeking wealth (chap. 5:1-6), and manifestation of the wrong kinds of wisdom (chap. 3:14-16). He admonishes all believers to covet divine wisdom: "If any of you lacks wisdom, he should ask God, who gives generously to all without finding fault, and it will be given to him" (chap. 1:5). "The wisdom from above is in the first place pure; and then peace-loving, considerate, and open for reason; it is straightforward and sincere, rich in mercy and in the kindly deeds that are its fruit" (chap. 3:17, N.E.B.). To use Paul's language in Galatians, it is the fruit of the Spirit (see chap. 5:22, 23).

Jesus pronounced His blessing upon the merciful (Matt. 5:7). James observed that divine wisdom expresses itself "in mercy and in the kindly deeds." And mercy will be the determining factor in the separation of the sheep and the goats (Matt. 25:31-46). "When the nations are gathered before Him, there will be but two classes, and their eternal destiny will be determined by what they have done or have neglected to do for Him in the person of the poor and the suffering."[11]

Divine wisdom will amply meet the threefold prescription for true Christianity James mentions in chapter 1:27. It will prevent contentions and strife (see chap. 4:1-12). As we are filled with God's Spirit and His love we will realize that "each has his place in the eternal plan of heaven. . . . Not more surely is the place prepared for us in the heavenly mansions than is the special place designated on earth where we are to work for God."[12] Guided by divine wisdom, we will aim to find and fill that niche. God's gift of wisdom will impart patience amid both trial and injustice (chaps. 1:12; 5:7), and remove wickedness, filth, lust, and covetousness from among us (chaps. 1:21; 4:2), as well as envy and pride (chaps. 3:14; 4:6).

James told his fellow Christians from the Jewish community that to know as much as his readers did and not implement it in ethical behavior was sin. "Anyone, then, who knows the good he ought to do and doesn't do it, sins" (verse 17). Genuine Christian faith demonstrates its reality in corresponding deeds. The true gospel will of necessity have ethical effects. "As the body without the spirit is dead, so faith without deeds is dead" (chap. 2:26).

---

[1] Herbert F. Stevenson, *James Speaks for Today* (Westwood, N.J.: Fleming H. Revell Co., 1966), p. 18.

[2] Archibald T. Robertson, *Word Pictures in the New Testament* (Nashville, Tenn.: Broadman Press, 1930-1933), Vol. VI, pp. 4, 5.

[3] John R. W. Stott, *Basic Introduction to the New Testament* (Grand Rapids, Mich.: William B. Eerdmans Pub. Co., 1979, pp. 103, 104.

[4] Ellen G. White, in *Review and Herald*, Nov. 9, 1897. (Italics supplied.)

[5] ———, *Testimonies*, vol. 8, p. 106.

[6] *Ibid.*, vol. 5, p. 43.

[7] ———, *Christ's Object Lessons* (Washington, D.C.: Review and Herald Pub. Assn., 1941), pp. 341, 342.

[8] ———, *Ibid.*, p. 335.

[9] *Ibid.*, p. 336.

[10] ———, *Testimonies*, vol. 9, p. 30.

[11] ———, *The Desire of Ages*, p. 637.

[12] ———, *Christ's Object Lessons*, pp. 326, 327.

Justification in Galatians and in James

Adam and Eve, our first parents, became sinners by eating forbidden fruit. They produced after their kind—sinners. All of us, are born into our world with sinful natures, are steeped in iniquity. "Your iniquities have made a gulf between you and your God" (Isa. 59:2, Jerusalem). In order to be saved or be able to live with God for eternity something or Someone must bridge the gulf, must put us right with God. Justification is imperative.

Unfortunately, much confusion surrounds this vital subject in the Christian community, including the Seventh-day Adventist Church. In 1890 Ellen G. White wrote that Adventists face a real danger of entertaining "false ideas of justification by faith" and "that Satan would work in a special manner to confuse the mind on this point."[1] Three years later she reiterated her concern. "Many are as ignorant as the very heathen in regard to the way in which a sinner can come to God and be justified before Him. . . . The important thing for them to know is, How can a sinner be justified before God?"[2]

Three Epistles in the New Testament speak of justification. Listed according to the probable date of their composition, they are James, Galatians, and

Romans. But when we examine them according to the depth with which they probe justification, we find the order reversed. In this chapter we shall briefly look at justification in Galatians and James.

What is justification? The noun *justification* appears only three times in the King James Version of the Bible, namely in Romans 4:25 and 5:16, 18. But the verb *justify* occurs many times both in the Old and the New Testament. In the New Testament it is translated from the Greek verb *dikaioō.* It may mean "make righteous," "declare righteous," "consider righteous," or "reckon righteous." Paul borrowed the figure of justification from the court of law and used it more than any other Bible writer. James referred to it in remonstrating against his readers who professed new life in Christ but failed to produce the corresponding fruit of Christian grace.

Before justification a person is unrighteous, unacceptable, or not set, or put, right with God. But through justification he is set right with God and becomes righteous or is regarded as righteous, and hence acceptable to God. The Greek verb for *justify* "therefore indicates *the act or process by which a man is brought into a right state as related to God.*"[3]

Our words *righteous* and *just* are both translations of *dikaios; righteousness,* of *dikaiosune;* and *a righteous act,* of *dikaiōma.* All come from the same root as *justify* and *justification.* But translating the Greek words, the English language uses words derived from different roots. Hence, the close connection between *just, justify, justification, righteous,* and *righteousness* does not readily show up in English as it does in the Greek original.

In discussing justification, both Paul and James refer to Abraham. Paul uses Abraham as an illustration of justification by faith without works, quoting from Genesis 15 the record of God's promise to him of a son.

Verse 6 reads, "Abraham believed the Lord, and he [God] credited it to him as righteousness." Commenting on it, Paul says, "And he received the sign of circumcision, a seal of the righteousness [justification] that he had by faith while he was still uncircumcised" (Rom. 4:11). Abraham trusted God's promise of a son even though at that time he did not understand how He would fulfill it, as is evident from Genesis 16. Nevertheless, God counted him righteous, or just, even with his immature faith.

James, on the other hand, uses Abraham as an illustration of justification by works, referring to his compliance with God's command to offer his son Isaac as a sacrifice on Mount Moriah (Gen. 22:1-14). "Was not our ancestor Abraham considered righteous [or just] for what he did when he offered his son Isaac on the altar?" (James 2:21).

Also, James offers Rahab's preservation of the lives of the two Israelite spies (Joshua 2) as an illustration of justification by works. "It was the same with the prostitute Rahab. She was put right with God through her actions, by welcoming the Israelite spies and helping them to escape by a different road" (James 2:25, T.E.V.). The pagan woman had come to believe in the God of the Israelites when she heard how He was working for them. "'For the Lord your God is God in heaven above and on the earth below'" (Joshua 2:11), she told them.

Some may wonder how Rahab, who had been justified, or put right with God, could blatantly lie to the messengers from the king of Jericho. Lying posed no problem to her. That difficulty arises only when we superimpose our Christian ethics on her pagan ones. Her culture did not regard lying as wrong, or sinful. But to expose people to death was. Even though God through His Spirit impressed her to follow her best knowledge and preserve the lives of the two spies, He did not at that time tell her that telling a falsehood was wrong. As she later became part of Israel, and one of the ancestors of Jesus (Matt. 1:5), she probably learned to shun untruths. But when faith moved her to protect the spies, lying posed no problem to her.

After using Rahab's deed of saving the spies as evidence of her justification by works, James says, "As the body without the spirit is dead, so faith without deeds is dead" (chap. 2:26).

In Galatians Paul comments, "Yet we know that a person is put right with God only through faith in Jesus Christ, never by doing what the Law requires. We, too, have believed in Christ Jesus in order to be put right with God through our faith in Christ, and not by doing what the Law requires. For no one is put right with God by doing what the Law requires" (chap. 2:16, T.E.V.).

As mentioned before, when Paul uses the word *law* in his Epistles to the Galatians and to the Romans, he has in mind both the ceremonial regulations of Judaism and the moral law as a means of salvation. As we read the Epistles to the Galatians and Romans today, when the ceremonial, or Mosaic, law is no longer a matter of concern, we do well to think of the law as all law, including the moral. And the moral law is just as helpless to justify, or put anyone right with God, as was the Mosaic law. That is not its purpose. (We will discuss its function in a later chapter.)

Thus we do violence to the intent of the words of both Paul and James and God when we set faith and works in opposition to each other in the experience of justification. They are not opposites. Rather, they are the two sides of man's experience in God. When Abraham first received the pledge of a son, he believed it. More than a decade later when God revealed that the son would come through Sarah, he again believed. And when God told him to sacrifice his son, he again trusted God and obeyed. Every time he did his part. He acted on the promise of a son by Sarah and later made the journey to

Mount Moriah to sacrifice his son of faith. Because his faith was real—tangible, living, dynamic—it produced action, impelled him to move in compliance with God's command. As a consequence of his active faith God accounted him righteous, or justified him, even when he failed to understand initially that Sarah would give birth to his son.

The apparent conflict between Paul and James in their discussion of justification rests—besides looking at different moments of Abraham's experience—on the impossibility of a human being's being able to discern the new life created by faith, through the Spirit, within a person. Each spring some of us plant small gardens in our backyards. One evening you are ready to plant peas. For a moment you hold a dozen seeds in your hand. The description on the seed packet guarantees 90 percent viability. You may wonder, as you look at the dozen peas, which are viable and which are dead. But you cannot tell. Neither can anyone else. The only way to find out is to plant them and see which germinate. But God knows even before you put them in the soil which have the germ of life in them and which do not.

So it is with the faith by which a person is justified, made righteous, or put right with God. Man cannot instantly discover whether a person is put right with his Lord through faith or not. God, on the other hand, knows the man's condition and his new attitude as soon as he commits himself to Him. Even though no outward evidence of his changed attitude toward Him has as yet appeared, He accounts him righteous. He recognizes the new life within.

James views justification from the human point of view. He says that when he sees what a person does, then he can know that the individual has faith, which indicates he or she stands justified, or put right with God. Paul looks at the same person from God's point of view. Our Lord can discern saving, or justifying, faith in someone even before works, or fruit, appear, just as He knows which peas are viable before they sprout. Man, on the other hand, must see the germination of the peas before he can tell the viable and the dead ones apart. So he also must observe evidence of justification before he knows for sure a person is justified.

Both Paul and James believed that faith and deeds go together in justification by faith. Speaking about Abraham, James concluded that "faith was working with [*sunergeō*] his works" (chap. 2:22, N.A.S.B.), or as *The New International Version* translates it, "His faith and his actions were working together, and his faith was made complete by what he did." James was trying to emphasize that we cannot separate faith and works in a genuine Christian experience. Mere profession of faith does not justify a man. Good works will inevitably follow justifying faith and validate it. "When we accept Christ, good works will appear as fruitful evidence that we are in the way of life."[4]

Many overweight persons say they believe in dieting. But mere mental assent to the idea does not help their obesity. Their belief, or faith, in dieting must result in action in order for them to reduce their weight. So it is with justification by faith unto salvation.

"James does not say that 'works' alone will declare a sinner righteous [see verse 24]. He is emphasizing that Abraham's works proved the genuineness of that faith which God had declared righteous."[5] Rather than substituting works *for* faith, James demands them as an evidence *of* faith. "Show me your faith without deeds, and I will show you my faith by what I do" (verse 18). His reasoning here rests on the solid basis of Hebrews 11, where the faith of all the Old Testament persons mentioned led to concrete actions and deeds.

Lenski observes that "in the Epistle of James 'faith alone' refers to a dead faith, one which even the devils have [chap. 2:19]; in this same epistle 'works' implies the presence of a faith that is indeed a faith. In Paul's letters 'faith (alone)' [Rom. 3:28] is this living faith mentioned by James; and in Paul's letters it is 'works of law' that are excluded, this spurious substitute for faith. James and Paul express the same truth: faith, faith, faith! James: not a dead faith which *is* no faith; Paul: no substitute for faith, there is none. How may we know when we have this real faith? James says: Investigate whether it has the real works."[6]

Forthrightly Lenski dismisses any conflict between Paul and James on the subject of justification. "The supposed clash between James and Paul is not based on facts. As James, so Paul knows of no verdict of acquittal for a faith that is dead and barren. Every subsequent verdict must include the works of faith. From the time of its creation true faith must attest itself by corresponding works. . . .

"There is no difference between James and Paul in regard to faith, good works, and declaring righteous. The difference that is sought in these terms with the object of harmonizing James and Paul fails of its good intent. Paul goes farther than James, for he is compelled to do so; he deals with the sinner's *first* acquittal, which James has no occasion to do; he also deals with *works of law*, which James does not need to treat. The readers of James were inclined to evade good works and to rely on a dead faith; those of Paul to rely on works of law without Christ and true faith in Him."[7]

John R. W. Stott agrees with Lenski. "Paul and James have been thought to contradict one another. . . . The contradiction between the two apostles is, however, purely imaginary. . . . The two men were given a different ministry but not a different message. They proclaimed the same gospel, but with a different emphasis.

"The reason for this different emphasis is not far to seek. They had a different set of false teachers in mind. Paul's opponents were the Jewish legalists. James's were the Jewish intellectualists. According to the legalists the way of salvaion was 'works'—moral and ceremonial acts performed in obedience to the law. According to the intellectualists the way of salvation was 'faith,' by which they meant mere orthodoxy of belief. To the legalists Paul argues that we are justified not by our own good works but through faith in Christ. To the intellectualists James argues that we are justified not by a barren orthodoxy (which even the demons possess—'and shudder'! chap. 2:19), but by works. Paul, however, is swift to add that the faith which saves issues inevitably in good works (Eph. 2:8-10; Gal. 5:6), while James affirms that the works which save spring naturally from a true faith (chap. 2:18). We are, in fact, saved neither by dead faith [verse 17] nor by dead works (Heb. 6:1; 9:14), but by a living faith which results in 'love and . . . good works' (chap. 10:24). We cannot be saved by works. Yet we cannot be saved without works. The place of works is not to earn salvation but to evidence it, not to procure salvation, but to prove it. The reality of one's faith is revealed in the quality of one's life. . . . Abraham's faith was of this calibre. He trusted God's promises, and therefore he obeyed God's command (James 2:21-24). He practiced 'the obedience of faith'—a phrase which Paul employs (Rom. 16:26). The Holy Spirit uses Paul to stress the faith which results in works and James to stress the works which result from faith."[8]

---

[1] Ellen G. White manuscript 36, 1890.

[2] Ellen G. White, *This Day With God* (Washington, D.C.: Review and Herald Pub. Assn., 1979), p. 18.

[3] Marvin R. Vincent, *Word Studies in the New Testament* (Grand Rapids, Mich.: William B. Eerdmans Pub. Co., 1946), Vol. III, p. 39.

[4] Ellen G. White, *Faith and Works* (Nashville, Tenn.: Southern Pub. Assn., 1979), p. 102.

[5] *The SDA Bible Commentary*, vol. 7, p. 522.

[6] R. C. H. Lenski, *The Interpretation of St. Paul's Epistle to the Romans* (Columbus, Ohio: Wartburg Press, 1945), p. 288.

[7] ———, *The Interpretation of the Epistle to the Hebrews and the Epistle of James* (Columbus, Ohio: Wartburg Press, 1946), pp. 589, 590.

[8] John R. W. Stott, *Basic Introduction to the New Testament*, pp. 104-106.

No Justification or Salvation by Law

Emphatically and repeatedly Paul states in both Galatians and Romans that the law will not justify anyone in the sight of God. Or to put it another way, "Now, it is clear that no one is put right with God by means of the Law" (Gal. 3:11, T.E.V.).

It is utterly impossible for a law that has already condemned the violator to death to put him into a life-giving relationship. No later good deeds, or works, however commendable, can free a lawbreaker from his death sentence; but a pardon may spare his life.

Paul uses the two sons of Abraham—Ishmael and Isaac—to set forth the contrast between the old and the new covenants (chap. 4:22-24). Human scheming and efforts apart from faith were responsible for Ishmael's birth. He represents the old covenant of attempted salvation by works without God's forgiving grace and enabling power. Isaac, on the other hand, was the direct result of God's promise and power. The child would not have been born apart from Abraham and Sarah's God-inspired faith in both the promise and power of God, and in their acting in accordance with their faith. Thus he symbolizes the new covenant of salvation by grace through faith in God's offer of forgiveness for sin and a change in the sinner's attitude from rebellion to willing obedience to God through the gift of the Holy Spirit.

At Sinai God wanted the children of Israel to become participants in the Abrahamic covenant of grace He had made with their forefather Abraham and the other patriarchs. The Abrahamic covenant is another name for "the eternal covenant" (Heb. 13:20). God introduced it to Adam and Eve in Eden when He said, " 'And I will put enmity between you and the woman, and between your offspring and hers; he will crush your head, and you will strike his heel' " (Gen. 3:15). "This covenant offered pardon and the assisting grace of God for future obedience through faith in Christ."[1]

The covenant embraced the plan of salvation. Paul says that "he [God] gave us this grace by means of Christ Jesus before the beginning of time" (2 Tim. 1:9, T.E.V.). The plan of salvation "was an unfolding of the principles that from eternal ages have been the foundation of God's throne."[2]

God tried to prepare the Israelites for this covenant of grace that reflects His love, mercy, and power. "He brought them down to the Red Sea—where, pursued by the Egyptians, escape seemed impossible—that they might realize their utter helplessness, their need of divine aid."[3]

Dry-shod, the fleeing Israelites had passed through the Red Sea, while the pursuing Egyptian army had perished in the returning waters (Ex. 14:27-30). Safe on the Sinai side of the Red Sea, they gratefully recognized that only God's powerful intervention had saved them from certain death, and they sang a song of praise to God (chap. 15:1-21). By God's direct intervention they later received food and water on their trek through the desert to Mount Sinai.

The Lord intended such miracles to impress them

with their need of divine help. But having lived for a long time "in the midst of idolatry and corruption, they had no true conception of the holiness of God, of the exceeding sinfulness of their own hearts, their utter inablity, in themselves, to render obedience to God's law, and their need of a Saviour."[4]

As He proposed His covenant to the Israelites, God again reminded them what He had done for them: " '"You yourselves have seen what I did to Egypt, and how I carried you on eagles' wings and brought you to myself. Now if you obey me fully and keep my covenant, then out of all nations you will be my treasured possession. Although the whole earth is mine, you will be for me a kingdom of priests and a holy nation"' " (chap. 19:4-6).

Unlimited possibilities for a prosperous and happy future lay before the Israelites. If they complied with God's condition of living according to His plan and will, the Lord Himself would uniquely work for them. He would set them "high above all the nations on earth," make them "the head, not the tail," and place them "at the top, never at the bottom" (Deut. 28:1, 13) of the community of nations.

" 'We will do everything the Lord has said' " (Ex. 19:8), the Israelites confidently responded. Later on they reiterated their promise and added, " 'We will obey' " (chap. 24:7). Moses sealed the agreement between them and God by sprinkling the people with " 'the blood of the covenant' " (verse 8). "The people did not realize the sinfulness of their own hearts, and that without Christ it was impossible for them to keep God's law; and they readily entered into covenant with God."[5] Thus originated the so-called old covenant.

It embraced the entire will of God for His people both as a nation and as individuals, including the moral law, or Ten Commandments, which actually formed its basis. But it also partook of the nature of a political alliance between God and Israel. God Himself would be their ally and assure them of victory in conflict with enemy nations. The Israelites, just having been slaves to the Egyptians, eagerly desired the political power and prominence He would bring them. And so, even before God had expressed the specifics of the agreement, the self-confident Israelites readily agreed to abide by everything the Lord would ask of them.

When God proposed His covenant to them at Sinai, His purpose with it was the same as that of the everlasting, or Abrahamic, covenant. But the Sinaitic covenant never achieved its goal, since the Israelites were aware neither of their need of forgiveness nor of the availability of enabling power to live in accordance with God's will. They self-confidently in their own strength promised to obey and do anything God would command. Thus "the terms of the 'old covenant' were Obey and live: 'If a man do, he shall live in them'; but 'cursed be he that confirmeth not all the words of this law to do them.'"[6]

If they had possessed the least spiritual perception, they would not have entered into such an arrangement with God for their salvation. As a matter of fact, the spiritual facet of the old covenant should never have been enacted. It was a cancer upon the eternal, or Abrahamic, covenant and came into existence only because of their spiritual blindness and self-conceit. They believed they could do God's will in their own strength and single-handedly work out their own salvation. In a sense it was forced upon God because the Israelites at Sinai were utterly oblivious of any need of divine help for their salvation. The newly formed nation believed that they could keep God's decrees and laws and live by them. Thus the spiritual part of the old covenant was based on self-salvation. Because of their condition God could do nothing except permit them to go ahead according to their own plan and stumble into failure.

A teacher quickly encounters the self-confident

assurance of certain students who are totally convinced they need no help. Although he offers them his assistance, they will not accept it. They believe they can master their assignments and solve any problems by themselves. The only option a teacher has in such a situation is to let the students go ahead on their own, and fail. Only after their own attempts prove futile are they willing and ready to accept anyone's aid.

Years ago I urged two college seniors to see me after class because they apparently had problems with the subject matter. But in spite of my repeated invitations, they never came. Both failed the nine-weeks test. Again I advised them to stop by my office—but to no avail. Naturally they did not pass the final exam. At last they both visited me—too late. Neither graduated in the spring commencement a few days later as they had planned.

The Israelites at Sinai were like those two students. Before they recognized they needed God's forgiveness and help, they had to fail. And fail they soon did. During Moses' absence they had Aaron make them a god of gold. (Ex. 32:1-6).

"Only a few weeks passed before they broke their covenant with God, and bowed down to worship a graven image. They could not hope for the favor of God through a covenant which they had broken; and now, seeing their sinfulness and their need of pardon, they were brought to feel their need of the Saviour revealed in the Abrahamic covenant and shadowed forth in the sacrificial offerings. Now by faith and love they were bound to God as their deliverer from the bondage of sin. Now they were prepared to appreciate the blessings of the new covenant."[7]

Both the old and the new covenants embraced the Ten Commandments. Under the old covenant the agreement rested on the frail foundation of human promises to "'do everything the Lord has said.'" The new, or everlasting covenant "is superior to the old one, and it is founded on better promises" (Heb. 8:6). In it God Himself assures humanity that " 'I will forgive their wickedness and will remember their sins no more,' " and " 'I will put my law in their minds and write it on their hearts. I will be their God, and they will be my people' " (Jer. 31:34, 33). Under the new covenant "Jesus has become the guarantee" (Heb. 7:22) of its fulfillment by forgiving our sins and writing His law on our hearts.

The new covenant is "the promise of forgiveness of sins and of the grace of God to renew the heart and bring it into harmony with the principles of God's law."[8] It is "simply an arrangement for bringing men again into harmony with the divine will, placing them where they could [can] obey God's law."[9]

For the Jews to enter into the old covenant and be "entrusted with the very words of God" (Rom. 3:2) was a great privilege. That was indeed glorious. But being written on tables of stone in the ark in the Most Holy Place of the tabernacle instead of in their characters, the law could only condemn to death or kill (see 2 Cor. 3:6-8). The same is true of us as long as God's law remains outside of us, as for instance on a plaque behind the pulpit, and not inscribed on our hearts.

Under the new covenant the law is no longer something external—on a plaque on a church wall. Rather it is now the motivation of our hearts and becomes a means of life through the Holy Spirit. So instead of being an agency of death, as the law was under the old covenant, it now brings righteousness. Excitedly Paul exclaims, "If the ministry that condemns man is glorious, how much more glorious is the ministry that brings righteousness!" (verse 9). "The Spirit of God works in the believer's soul, enabling him to advance from one line of obedience to another."[10]

The old covenant attempted to provide justification and salvation by the law, since the Israelites perceived no need of divine help. And neither justification nor salvation is possible by the law—neither the Mosaic law, with circumcision, nor the ten-commandment law.

No sinner—and all human beings are sinners by breaking God's law—can come into a right relationship with God through the aid of a broken law. A transgressed law only condemns.

"The law demands righteousness, and this the sinner owes to the law; but he is incapable of rendering it. The only way in which he can attain to righteousness is through faith. By faith he can bring to God the merits of Christ, and the Lord places the obedience of His Son to the sinner's account. Christ's righteousness is accepted in place of man's failure, and God receives, pardons, justifies, the repentant, believing soul, treats him as though he were righteous, and loves him as He loves His Son. This is how faith is accounted righteousness."[11]

"He who is trying to reach heaven by his own works in keeping the law, is attempting an impossibility. Man cannot be saved without obedience, but his works should not be of himself; Christ should work in him to will and to do of His good pleasure. If a man could save himself by his own works, he might have something in himself in which to rejoice. . . . All that man can do without Christ is polluted with selfishness and sin; but that which is wrought through faith is acceptable to God."[12]

Every person saved in the kingdom of God will be there because God, by His love and the grace of our Lord Jesus Christ in dying for us, justified him, or put him right with Him. God's eternal kingdom will have no self-saved people. All the redeemed will agree with the four living creatures and the twenty-four elders when they praise Jesus, saying, " 'You are worthy . . . because you were slain, and with your blood you purchased men for God from every tribe and language and people and nation' " (Rev. 5:9).

---

[1] Ellen G. White, *Patriarchs and Prophets*, p. 370.
[2] ———, *The Desire of Ages*, p. 22.
[3] ———, *Patriarchs and Prophets*, p. 371.
[4] *Ibid.*
[5] *Ibid.*, pp. 371, 372.
[6] *Ibid.*, p. 372.
[7] *Ibid.*
[8] *Ibid.*
[9] *Ibid.*, p. 371.
[10] ———, in *Review and Herald*, Nov. 1, 1892.
[11] *The SDA Bible Commentary*, Ellen G. White Comments, on Rom. 4:3-5, p. 1073.
[12] Ellen G. White, *Selected Messages*, book 1, (Washington, D.C.: Review and Herald Pub. Assn., 1958), p. 364.

The Purpose of the Law

Some years ago I spent a few days with other travelers in a tourist camp at the Amboseli Game Reserve on the Tanzania border in southern Kenya. The semidesert spread out in front of our cabins, and in the distance the snowcapped top of the mighty Kilimanjaro appeared through the high clouds for a few hours each day. A few hundred feet away from our cabins I found signs reading, "Do not walk beyond this point; the lions have the right-of-way." During the day we traveled around in sightseeing buses accompanied by armed guards. We saw a small pride of lions, herds of elephants, giraffes, zebras, and, as it appeared, innumerable antelopes and gazelles and wildebeests, plus a few slinking cheetahs, strutting ostriches, and trees filled with vultures.

One afternoon we spotted a solitary lion sleepily lying close to a giraffe in whose throat it had gouged a large hole. For the first time I understood why the lion has received the name king of beasts. All the other animals—including the huge elephants and tall giraffes—ran away from us when we approached. That lion, however, seemed to ignore us completely, hardly moving a muscle, although we passed within thirty feet of where it rested by its prey. At night we could also hear the distant roar of the lions. Because we were in lion country, our safety depended upon our following the instructions our guides gave us.

Our world is also lion country. It became such when God had to expel Satan with his angels from heaven. "The great dragon was hurled down—that ancient serpent called the devil or Satan, who leads the whole world astray. He was hurled to the earth, and his angels with him" (Rev. 12:9). Ever since, he has prowled "around like a roaring lion looking for someone to devour" (1 Peter 5:8).

God knew Satan's intent and so took precaution to protect Adam and Eve and their posterity from his sly onslaughts. In His loving concern for His earth children He built a fence of protection around them.

Years ago while teaching at a Midwestern college, I passed by a certain house each morning on my way to classes. Its backyard was fenced with chicken wire. The people who lived there had no chickens—undoubtedly a city ordinance prohibited keeping them in that zone. But often as I walked home for lunch on warm summer days I noticed two small boys—about 3 and 5 years of age—playing inside the fence. A busy street ran by the house, and cars sped back and forth on it in a continuous stream. Out of love for their two boys, the parents had erected the fence to protect and shield the youngsters from the danger of their running out on the street.

God's fence of protection around Adam and Eve was His law. At Creation "its precepts were written upon their hearts."[1] In sin-free Eden the prohibition of God's law was simple: Adam and Eve had to show their loyalty to God just by refraining from eating of the tree of the knowledge of good and evil (Gen. 2:16, 17). To the fruit of all the other trees in the garden they had free access, but sampling from the tree of knowledge would result only in disaster—death.

"The tree of knowledge had been made a test of their obedience and their love to God. The Lord had seen fit to lay upon them but one prohibition as to the use of all that was in the garden; but if they should disregard His will in this particular, they would incur the guilt of transgression. Satan was not to follow them with continual temptations; he could have access to them only at the forbidden tree."[2]

But Adam and Eve broke down God's fence by stumbling into sin. Then He articulated the principles of the law, written upon their hearts at Creation, in greater detail. "The law of Jehovah, dating back to creation, was comprised in the two great principles, 'Thou shalt love the Lord thy God with all thy heart, and with all thy soul, and with all thy mind, and with all thy strength: this is the first commandment. And the second is like, namely this, Thou shalt love thy neighbour as thyself. There is none other commandment greater than these.' . . . After the transgression of Adam the principles of the law were not changed, but were definitely arranged and expressed to meet man in his fallen condition."[3] God intended the law to help Adam and Eve more easily detect Satan's temptations and enable them to overcome them.

Afterward "Adam taught his descendants the law of God, and it was handed down from father to son through successive generations. . . . The law was preserved by Noah and his family, and Noah taught his descendants the Ten Commandments."[4] Of Abraham, God stated that he " 'obeyed me and kept my requirements, my commands, my decrees and my laws' " (Gen. 26:5).

During their stay in Egypt the knowledge of God's will as expressed in the law almost faded from the enslaved Israelites. For that reason He gave them the law in written form at Sinai. In addition to the moral law, expressed in the Ten Commandments, He also provided them a civil law, since they were now to be a nation. To guide them in their religious life and services, He supplied the ceremonial law. It contained elaborate rules pertaining to the sanctuary (Temple) services, including animal and other offerings. Many of them were object lessons in the plan of salvation to help them understand His will and plan more easily. He also gave them sanitary laws to safeguard their health.

As used in the Bible, the term *law* therefore has several different meanings. It does mean the Ten Commandments. The apostle Paul in the New Testament uses it in that sense, as for instance in Romans 7:7, where he wrote, "What shall we say, then? Is the law sin? Certainly not! Indeed I would not have known what sin was except through the law." More widely, *law* refers to the entire Pentateuch, or the first five books of the Bible. That concept embraces the Israelite civil laws and the ritual precepts governing their worship and sacrifices, as well as the sanitary regulations. In still another sense, *law* refers to the whole Old Testament. Paul uses the word that way as we see in Romans 3, where he quotes from both Isaiah and Psalms and speaks of them as "the law." Even beyond that, *law* in the Bible may refer to the entire will of God as revealed to the Jews.

In this chapter, however, we will restrict the term to the moral law, or God's will as expressed in the Ten Commandments. And the Decalogue, like all the laws God gave, was intended to save men and women from evil and mishaps.

Several years ago I was driving along a section-line road on the wheat plains of North Dakota to reach a friend's farm. It was a road used almost exclusively by the local farmers. I had headed out to the farm on one road, but decided to return to the highway by taking another. As I traveled up a slight incline, it appeared to me as if the road went on indefinitely along the straight section line. Suddenly the terrain leveled off, and dead ahead lay a ninety-degree right turn at the end of the section. With my speed it was impossible to navigate such a curve, and I shot off the road into the deep ditch. My friend had to use his tractor to pull my car out. The absence of road signs had contributed to my misfortune. Local farmers who knew the road and its curves well had not deemed any signs necessary.

Ever since that dismal visit to the ditch, I have appreciated road signs that indicate safe speeds for particular sections of a road. No longer do I regard them as impudent restrictions on my freedom. When I see a sign telling me that a safe speed is thirty miles per hour, I am actually grateful. I recognize it is erected for my safety, happiness, and preservation of life itself.

God's law is comparable to such signs. Thus it admonishes, " 'You shall not give false testimony against your neighbor' " (Ex. 20:16), lest your acquaintances begin to distrust, dislike, and hate you. The psalmist had learned to heed God's road signs along life's highway. "I have hidden your word in my heart that I might not sin against you" (Ps. 119:11), he exclaimed. Truly "there will grow in the receptive mind a familiarity with divine things which will be as a barricade against the temptations of the enemy."[5]

But the law does not stop with just protecting and warning against danger. It also points out what is wrong with my life and practices when I deviate from God's plan. We have many practices common among us today that God labels as sin and hence unacceptable in His sight. For example, we handle truthfulness lightly. One good friend of mine—and a good moral person at that—once confessed to me, "I had to lie. If I had not, everything we had planned would have collapsed."

Marital unfaithfulness is also prevalent in the society in which we live. Even some Christians have come to the place where they see nothing wrong in it. But the Word of God says, " 'You shall not commit adultery' " (Ex. 20:14).

Adultery in this text means not only marital unfaithfulness but sexual gratification of any kind outside of marriage.

The apostle Paul makes it clear that it is the purpose of the law to identify sin. Not to justify a sinner, but to pinpoint sin. "Through the law we become conscious of sin" (Rom. 3:20). "Indeed I would not have known what sin was except through the law" (chap. 7:7).

James compares the law to a mirror, or a looking glass (chap. 1:22-25). Most of us probably glance into a mirror many times a day to ascertain that our appearance is acceptable. The mirror in itself does not produce any changes in how we look. It only reflects our image and exposes any flaws in it. When I finished shaving with my electric shaver this morning, I stared into the mirror. The mirror did not remove the remaining whiskers. It only pointed out where I had missed them. By showing me that I did not have a clean shave, it helped me go after the remaining places in order to improve my appearance.

So it is with the law of God. It directs our attention to our lack of harmony with God's will. By doing so, it hopefully prompts us to seek help from Jesus. As we come to Him, He forgives us for our departures from His will and washes away all blemishes on our characters with His shed blood.

Paul points out this very function of the law when he speaks of it as "our schoolmaster to bring us unto Christ" (Gal. 3:24, K.J.V). Law here refers to the totality of the Jewish law—moral, ceremonial, civil, and sanitary—which were all to aid and guide the Jews "until God's provision for salvation by faith should be 'revealed' with the coming of Christ."[6]

William Barclay points out that the Greek *paidagōgos*, translated "schoolmaster," does not refer to a child's teacher, but rather to the trusted servant who took the child to and from school. "He had nothing to do with the actual teaching of the child, but it was his duty to take him in safety to the school and deliver him to the teacher. That—said Paul—was like the function of the law. It was there to lead a man to Christ. It could not take him into Christ's presence, but it could take him into a position where he himself might enter."[7]

Ellen White wrote: " 'The law was our schoolmaster to bring us unto Christ, that we might be justified by faith.' In this scripture, the Holy Spirit through the apostle is speaking especially of the moral law. The law reveals sin to us, and causes us to feel our need of Christ and to flee unto Him for pardon and peace by exercising repentance toward God and faith toward our Lord Jesus Christ."[8]

The broken law as a truant officer leads—urges, compels—a sinner to come to Christ for help in his or her desperate need. It sharpens the sense of need and exercises mental discipline over those who are inclined to or are guilty of misconduct.

After the law has prompted us to flee to Christ for help and healing, it aims to aid us to cope successfully with all the problems of life. As a youth in Sweden, I often had occasion to use a yoke. A yoke is a frame of wood hollowed out to fit the neck and shoulders, extending twelve to fifteen inches on each side of the body. People use it to carry pails suspended by chains from the ends. Nowadays Vermonters use it to carry maple sap out of the woods in the spring.

When my brothers and I carried water to the garden, we invariably used a yoke. We could haul two six-gallon pails without undue effort. Even with such a load, I could put my hands in my pockets as I walked along. The yoke made the otherwise heavy burden seem lighter and enabled me to carry it more easily and comfortably.

The yoke helps oxen pull loads more easily. It would be possible to hitch up the animals to a wagon by placing ropes over their necks and across their chests. Pulling a load with such an improvised harness, however, would cruelly lacerate the oxen, inasmuch as the ropes under the pressure of the load would cut into their flesh.

Even though the word *yoke* today ordinarily carries a connotation of oppression or burdensome toil, its purpose is the exact opposite. It actually eases one's load. I recall how happy my brothers and I were to use a yoke when we transported those big six-gallon pails. It would have been a most arduous task to carry them without the yoke. But with it the burden became bearable.

God's law is a yoke to help us bear the burdens of life. Therefore Jesus invites us, " 'Come to me, all you who are weary and burdened, and I will give you rest. Take my yoke upon you and learn from me' " (Matt. 11:28, 29). And Ellen G. White declares that "the yoke . . . is the law of God."[9]

God gave the law for man's good. Moses anciently told the Israelites, " 'The Eternal ordered us to keep all these rules, and to reverence the Eternal our God, for our own lasting good, that he might keep us alive' " (Deut. 6:24, Moffatt). The Lord meant for it to preserve human life. But Paul states in Romans 7:10 "that the very commandment that was intended to bring life actually brought death."

Today most American houses are wired for electricity. Electricity enhances the tenants' comfort and enjoyment. But although we run electricity into our homes for our good, we can turn that same power to our harm and hurt. My house has some appliances that require 220-volt current to run through their wires. Instead of using that current to operate a machine, I could create, and touch, a live wire. The result would be lethal. The contractor did not install the 220-volt circuits to kill me or anyone else living in the house, but to furnish adequate power for the power tools and other devices needing that much current. The high voltage can destroy me, however, if I do not restrict it to its intended purpose.

So God in the beginning gave the law to Adam and Eve for their good—to preserve them alive. But by their misusing it, the very thing that God had designed to preserve their life became a means unto death. He bestowed the law to protect, not to hurt or kill.

Shortly after Mae and I were married, we lived for two years on the plains of North Dakota. When we arrived there, the rarity of fences immediately struck me. But even though fences were scarce, I invariably noticed, as I began to visit farm families in their homes, a small patch surrounded with chicken wire close to each farmhouse. Soon I learned the enclosure was not for the chickens or the turkeys. The farmers allowed them to roam the farmyard and nearby fields. On the contrary, the fence encompassed a small garden where the farmer's wife raised kitchen vegetables and flowers. The fence was not to confine cattle or fowl to the area, but rather to protect the garden from marauding animals. The plants were safe inside the wire fencing.

So God intended that people—you and I—should be safe and secure inside the fence of His love—the Ten Commandments. The Israelites on the plains of Moab, just before their crossing of the Jordan, were safe inside their fence. Despite Balaam's attempt to bring a curse upon Israel, he was unable to do so, and stated under inspiration, "He [God] has discovered no iniquity in Jacob and has seen no mischief in Israel. The Lord their God is with them, acclaimed among them as king" (Num. 23:21, N.E.B.). God's fence of love protected them until they broke it. When they did so by committing fornication and worshiping idols with the Moabites, a dreadful plague fell upon them (chap. 25:1-9).

As true followers of our Lord Jesus, we will not despise and downgrade His law. Rather, we will choose to regard it as it actually is, as a gift of His love to us to help us live safely and happily in our world, and as a guide to eternal life. We shall ask Jesus to open our eyes so that we "may see wonderful things" (Ps. 119:18) in His law and come to the place where we exclaim with the psalmist, "Oh, how I love your law! I meditate on it all day long" (verse 97).

"In obedience to God's law, man is surrounded as with a hedge and kept from the evil. He who breaks down this divinely erected barrier at one point has destroyed its power to protect him; for he has opened a way by which the enemy can enter to waste and ruin."[10]

---

[1] Ellen G. White, *Patriarchs and Prophets*, p. 363.

[2] *Ibid.*, p. 53.

[3] *The SDA Bible Commentary*, revised edition (Washington, D.C.: Review and Herald Pub. Assn., 1978), Ellen G. White Comments, on Ex. 20:1-17, p. 1104.

[4] Ellen G. White, *Patriarchs and Prophets*, p. 363.

[5] ———, *Counsels to Parents and Teachers* (Mountain View, Calif.: Pacific Press Pub. Assn., 1943), p. 172.

[6] *The SDA Bible Commentary*, vol. 6, p. 961.

[7] William Barclay, *The Letters to the Galatians and Ephesians*, p. 31.

[8] Ellen G. White, *Selected Messages*, book 1, p. 234.

[9] ———, *The Desire of Ages*, p. 329.

[10] ———, *Thoughts From the Mount of Blessing* (Mountain View, Calif.: Pacific Press Pub. Assn., 1956), p. 52.

Led by the Spirit

The Galatian Christians had begun in the Spirit, but Judaizing teachers had entered their midst and confused them. Because of their influence, the Galatians concluded that they could gain salvation by lawkeeping. "How can you be so foolish!" Paul exclaimed. "You began by God's Spirit; do you now want to finish by your own power?" (Gal. 3:3, T.E.V.). Or as paraphrased by Kenneth Nathaniel Taylor, "Then have you gone completely crazy? For if trying to obey the Jewish laws never gave you spiritual life in the first place, why do you think that trying to obey them now will make you stronger Christians?" (T.L.B.).

No law can beget children. Neither can the law of God bring about the new birth. To become children of God, we must be born "through the word of truth" (James 1:18). Peter says that we are "born again, not of perishable seed, but of imperishable, through the living and enduring word of God" (1 Peter 1:23). Luther observed that the Word "is the divine womb in which we are conceived, carried, born, reared, et cetera."[1]

Before a sinner chooses to come to God and trust Him as His Father, Jesus through the Holy Spirit stands at his heart's door and pleads for permission to come in (Rev. 3:20). "The Spirit and the bride say, 'Come!'" (chap. 22:17). He appeals to all to accept reconciliation to God (2 Cor. 5:20). On Calvary Jesus removed every barrier to a relationship of friendship and peace between His Father and the sinner. When the sinner chooses to trust himself to God, the Lord then confirms that relationship by giving him His Holy Spirit (chap. 1:22). Faith in God's promise of reconciliation brings us into a father-son relationship with Him. And the Spirit is God's conferred sign that the believer is His and belongs to Him.

The Judaizers led the Galatian believers to doubt they had sonship if they neglected the ceremonial law. But Paul attempted to convince them that sonship does not depend on circumcision, but on their acceptance of and having been "baptized into Christ" and having "been clothed with Christ" (Gal. 3:27). A more reliable evidence of their being children of God than circumcision, he said, was the gift of the Holy Spirit. Circumcision, with the practice of the ceremonial law, did not make them sons and daughters of God. Faith had already made them such (John 1:12). The Holy Spirit dwelling within them assured them of their new status. "Because you are sons, God sent the Spirit of his Son into our hearts, the Spirit who calls out, '*Abba*, Father'" (Gal. 4:6; cf. Rom. 8:15, 16). *Abba* is a transliteration of the Aramaic word for father, and *Father* here is a translation of the Greek word for father. Paul probably used both terms in consideration of the fact that the Galatian church included both Gentiles and Jews.

Satan continuously seeks to make us doubt that we are God's children. He tries to convince us that we do not belong to Him, but that as sinners God is angry with us and will damn us for eternity. For that very reason our Lord has given us His Spirit. In every moment of temptation to doubt that we are sons and daughters of

God, the presence of the Holy Spirit reassures us that we belong to Him. When we first believed we "were marked in him with a seal, the promised Holy Spirit" (Eph. 1:13).

Satan knows that if he can cause us to question that we belong to God, we will be easy prey for discouragement and defeat. He tried to instill the same uncertainty in the mind of Jesus when he came to Him in the wilderness of temptation and said, " 'If you are the Son of God . . .' " (Matt. 4:6).

As Christians we will make it a habit not to question or doubt God's acceptance. We must never succumb to the temptation to decide to whom we belong on the basis of our feeling of unworthiness. Rather we will exercise hope, remembering that God is favorably disposed toward us. As long as we remain in our faith relationship to Jesus, we have His unbreakable promise that " 'whoever comes to me I will never drive away' " (John 6:37). The greatest blasphemy we can commit is to doubt God's promises.

Knowing that they were sons and daughters of God by the indwelling of the Spirit, Paul admonished the Galatian believers, "Walk in the Spirit, and ye shall not fulfil the lust of the flesh" (Gal. 5:16, K.J.V.). " 'Walk' is the favorite Biblical metaphor to describe the whole course of man's life, including his conduct toward God and his treatment of his fellow men."[2]

To "walk in the Spirit" sums up Paul's imperative of the Christian life. Modern versions make the passage even more clear. "What I say is this: let the Spirit direct your lives, and you will not satisfy the desires of the human nature" (T.E.V.), or "I mean this: if you are guided by the Spirit you will not fulfil the desires of your lower nature" (N.E.B.).

Paul shows that justification by faith is a determining factor and results in a changed life. It directs human behavior into a new way. His own life illustrated it. The Spirit effects the change. Christianity is essentially a way of life, " 'that Way' " (Acts 24:14, T.E.V.), or " 'the new way' " (N.E.B.; see chaps. 9:2; 19:9, 23; 22:4). Justification by faith is the beginning of a new life in Christ that provides continuity, guidance, and assurance of victory in the task of coping with the daily struggles against evil. This experience will immunize a believer against gratifying the desires of his lower nature and enable him to bear the fruit of the Spirit as the indwelling Spirit leads him.

"Through the work of the Holy Spirit, the sanctification of the truth, the believer becomes fitted for the courts of heaven; for Christ works within us, and His righteousness is upon us. Without this no soul will be entitled to heaven. We would not enjoy heaven unless qualified for its holy atmosphere by the influence of the Spirit and the righteousness of Christ."[3]

Paul advised the Galatians to continue what they had been doing: "Do not stop or change your course now but persevere in the good under the guidance of the Holy Spirit." Then he promised them that if they did so, "you will not fulfil [or carry out] the desires of your lower nature" (Gal. 5:16, N.E.B.). In other words, if the Christian allows the Holy Spirit to direct, or fill, his life, then He will prevent the opposite force, represented by the flesh or the person's sinful human nature or his "lower nature," from achieving its goal. In that way "the lust of the flesh" (or "the desires of your lower nature") will not be able to assert itself.

Every person is a battlefield on which two adversary forces contend. "For what our human nature wants is opposed to what the Spirit wants, and what the Spirit wants is opposed to what our human nature wants. These two are enemies" (verse 17, T.E.V.).

If a person does not positively ally himself and place his will on the side of the Holy Spirit, the evil impulses of his "lower nature" will be victorious over the good. No one by himself will be able to carry out his good intentions or resist his evil drives. He will be defeated.

But faith comes to our aid, for it "will control the affections and the impulses of the heart."[4] The only hope of every Christian for victory over baser passions is faith, or trust, in God's help, which we receive through the Spirit. The Spirit prompts us to do what we know is right, and to the willing believer He gives power to follow His biddings.

The cravings of the body may not be sinful in themselves, but the person's manner of fulfilling them may be outside the pale of God's will and thus be sinful. A hungry person craves food. The body is not particular how we take care of that need. Stolen food or items not intended by God for food will satisfy the body's demands. The same is true about the God-given sexual drive. It is not sinful in itself, but the time, place, and one's relationship to the person with whom he or she resolves the prompting may make it sinful.

The Spirit-led Christian experiences no oppression under the law. Paul triumphantly concludes, "But if ye be led of the Spirit, ye are not under the law" (verse 18, K.J.V.). This phrase in Galatians and in Romans we can understand to mean either of two things. One, that the believer is not under law as a method of salvation (as the Jews in the day of Paul used it), but under grace as a method of salvation; or two, that the believer is not under the condemnation of the law, but under God's forgiving grace. Probably Paul had the first definition in mind. He was not arguing freedom from either the ceremonial or the moral law, but rather that acceptance by God, or justification, is by faith and not by works, and that Christians are dead to the law as a mode of salvation.

Paul was free from the oppressive demands of the ceremonial law. To him they were a matter of indifference. He might circumcise Timothy (Acts 16:1-3) or at times observe some of them from choice, as he did at Cenchrea and later at Jerusalem (chaps. 18:18; 21:17-

26), but never from the belief that God demanded them for his salvation. Thus he refused to have Titus circumcised, even though some delegates to the Jerusalem Council apparently urged it (Gal. 2:3). While indeed free, Paul yet chose to fit into whatever place or society he happened to be in order to win men and women to Christ.

Furthermore, Paul was neither under nor oppressed by the moral law. In Galatians 2:19 he states: "For through the law I died to the law so that I might live for God." The Greek here has no article before *law*. As such, *law* here includes everything that merits the name, rather than denoting solely either the Mosaic regulations or the Ten Commandments. Ellen G. White, commenting about the law in Galatians, said, "I am asked concerning the law in Galatians. What is the schoolmaster to bring us to Christ? I answer: Both the ceremonial and the moral code of ten commandments."[5]

Jesus, in Matthew 5:41, reminded the Jews that the Romans had reserved the right for themselves to impress a Jew into service for them. A Roman soldier could compel someone to carry his baggage a mile, a prerogative the soldiers used when they drafted Simon of Cyrene to help with Jesus' cross (chap. 27:32). As Simon bore the cross he was not free, but a slave. So were all Jews who carried a Roman burden for that one mile. Thus Jesus told them to go the second mile. The Jew who did that was no longer a slave, but the free master of his own action.

The same is true in our relationship to God's law. As long as a Christian focuses his attention on trying to fulfill it, he senses its oppressiveness and is its slave. Eight of the Ten Commandments are couched in negations: not to steal, not to murder, et cetera. They express minimum requirements. Those who concentrate on negatives lead a joyless life. Although they may claim to be Christians, really they are not. When the Holy

Spirit lives within the believer, however, he is no longer concerned about minimums. Instead of stealing, he helps and gives, and instead of killing, he lets live and helps others to live. As long as we Christians fix our eyes on the requirements, we too are slaves. But "if you are led by the Spirit, you are not under law" (Gal. 5:18), because we then do gladly and willingly by free choice what God wants. Luther wrote that "we cannot live to God unless we have died to the law. Therefore we must climb up to this heavenly attitude, in order that we may establish for certain that we are far above the law, in fact, that we are completely dead to the law."[6]

Luther was correct. A Christian will "climb up to this heavenly attitude." "In heaven, service is not rendered in the spirit of legality. When Satan rebelled against the law of Jehovah, the thought that there was a law came to the angels almost as an awakening to something unthought of. In their ministry the angels are not as servants, but as sons. . . . Obedience is to them no drudgery. Love for God makes their service a joy. So in every soul wherein Christ, the hope of glory, dwells, His words are reechoed, 'I delight to do thy will, O my God: yea, thy law is within my heart.' Psalm 40:8."[7] Thank God, we are not servants but children. "See how much the Father has loved us! His love is so great that we are called God's children—and so, in fact, we are" (1 John 3:1, T.E.V.).

God does not want us to be slaves. He desires us to be His free children. We are so when we choose to go the second mile. Life then becomes pleasurable and enjoyable.

Instead of bringing salvation, the law places a curse upon every person born into the world. Although born as a tabula rasa—a clean sheet of paper—every person in this world of sin soaks it up as blotting paper soaks up liquid. And to such a being, the law becomes a curse. It condemns him to death. The law puts us all under a curse. But Jesus stepped into our place and took it upon

Himself. He who was without sin assumed our sin and became a curse for us. And "by becoming a curse for us Christ has redeemed us from the curse that the Law brings" (Gal. 3:13, T.E.V.).

If a person could have lived with a right attitude toward God and His law from birth and never sinned, then the law would have justified and saved him. "As the scripture says, 'Whoever *does* everything the Law requires will live'" (verse 12, T.E.V.). But that has happened in the experience of only one human being—Jesus. And He was able to do that because He was born through the Holy Spirit (Luke 1:35) and was filled with the fullness of the Spirit from His birth (John 3:34). When He came to the end of His life, He said, "'The ruler of this world is coming. He has no power over me; but I do as the Father has commanded me'" (chap. 14:30, 31, R.S.V.). The law had no claim on Jesus because He had always kept it. Moses, on the other hand, by virtue of sin, really belonged to the devil. Consequently Satan contested when Michael, or Christ, resurrected and took him to heaven (Jude 9). Jesus was different. Thus He could absorb the curse that should have fallen on us. As a result He died in our stead.

Our justification and salvation can come only through Jesus, who volunteered to die in our place. "God made him who had no sin to be sin for us, so that in him we might become the righteousness of God" (2 Cor. 5:21). "We have been put right with God through faith" and "have peace with God through our Lord Jesus Christ" (Rom. 5:1, T.E.V.).

"Christians do not become righteous by doing righteous works," Luther said, "but once they have become justified by faith [made righteous] in Christ, they do righteous works."[8] "The doers of the law are believers, who, having received the Holy Spirit, fulfill the law and love God and their neighbor. Thus the 'doer of the law' . . . is one who, having already become a person through faith, then becomes a doer. . . . Those who have been made righteous do righteous things. . . . Therefore we, being justified by faith, do good works, through which, as 2 Peter 1:10 says, our call and election are confirmed and made more certain day by day."[9]

"Therefore 'to do' is first to believe and so, through faith, to keep the law. For we must receive the Holy Spirit; illumined and renewed by Him, we begin to keep the law, to love God and our neighbor."[10]

A Christian will live and relate differently to the problems of life than will his friends and acquaintances in the world. "If a man does not keep pace with his companion, perhaps it is because he hears a different drummer," Thoreau observed. "Let him step to the music which he hears, however measured or far away."[11]

Most people reading, discussing, and writing about the Epistle to the Galatians gain and give the impression that its thrust is justification by faith. The book does mention justification eight times (in the King James Version; other versions may use other terms for the identical idea in the original), all within its first three chapters except once in chapter 5. But Galatians mentions the Spirit sixteen times, twice as often as it refers to justification, and preponderantly in the latter part of the Epistle.

Paul began his Epistle to the Galatians with a discussion of justification by faith, or how a sinner can come into a right relationship to God. But he ends it by showing that a justified person is continually guided by the Spirit.

The salient point of Paul's Epistle to the Galatians is therefore that the Christian life begins in the Spirit and remains constantly Spirit-directed. This means freedom from both the oppression of sin and guilt and the coercive pressure of the law itself. The apostle sought to stir up the Galatian believers to their freedom in Christ and to live joyfully and march to the music that came to them through the Holy Spirit from their Leader at the throne of the universe. So not justification by faith, but the resultant life in and through the Spirit, is the thrust of Paul's letter to the Galatians.

---

[1] Jaroslav Pelikan (ed.), *Luther's Works*, vol. 26, p. 392.
[2] From Raymond T. Stamm, in *The Interpreter's Bible*, vol. 10, p. 560. Used by permission of Abingdon Press.
[3] Ellen G. White, *Selected Messages*, book 1, p. 395.
[4] ———, *Faith and Works*, p. 100.
[5] ———, *Selected Messages*, book 1, p. 233.
[6] Pelikan, *op. cit.*, p. 156.
[7] Ellen G. White, *Thoughts From the Mount of Blessing*, p. 109.
[8] Pelikan, *op. cit.*, p. 256.
[9] *Ibid.*, pp. 259, 260.
[10] *Ibid.*, p. 255.
[11] Henry David Thoreau, *Walden and "Civil Disobedience"* (New York: New American Library, 1960), p. 216.

Joy in the Lord

Both the Epistle to the Galatians and James's letter point out that those who belong to God and Jesus will possess joy. According to Paul, the first manifestation of Spirit-inspired love is joy (Gal. 5:22). That seems natural to us from our knowledge of human relations where true love invariably produces delight and happiness. A young woman told me on her wedding day that she had never been so happy as she had been since she met the man she was about to marry. Her love for him produced joy. In the same way a personal love relationship with Jesus will bring even greater gladness.

God-inspired joy is not necessarily dependent on ideal external circumstances. James believed that a follower of Jesus will be joyful in spite of trials: "Consider it pure joy, my brothers, whenever you face trials of many kinds" (chap. 1:2).

Christian joy will flourish amid favorable conditions, but it is not dependent on them. It is rather like a pine tree that survives close to the tree line high up on a mountain, swept by ferocious, snow-filled winds. Despite its hostile surroundings, it grows because its roots are anchored securely in the crevices between the rocks. So a Christian may possess quiet inward joy despite difficult circumstances, because he knows his life and eternal security are firmly affixed in the Rock of Ages.

The apostles possessed such joy. They rejoiced "because they had been counted worthy of suffering disgrace for the Name" (Acts 5:41) of Jesus. Paul and Silas expressed it when they sang praises to God in the prison at Philippi after a severe flogging at the order of the city magistrates (Acts 16:22-25). All these ambassadors of the gospel felt joy, in spite of adversity and suffering, because they knew their names were " 'written in heaven' " (Luke 10:20). They "possessed a Presence who acted like an inward spring of water—such as Jesus promised to the woman of Samaria at the well (John 4:14)—whose source is deep in the mountains of God."[1] Paul and Silas knew that Jesus was with them even in prison. Aware of His presence, they possessed good courage and could sing.

Paul's converts at Thessalonica possessed such joy (1 Thess. 1:6) amid physical persecution (Acts 17:1-9). A. T. Robertson says that " 'this paradox of experience' . . . shines along the pathway of martyrs and saints of Christ."[2] As someone has said, "How men treat us will make little difference when we know we have God's approval." It is such assurance that produces inward peace and joy.

Trials and temptations are tests. A person is not allowed to sit for a school test unless he has qualified. Thus trials and temptations verify man's exalted state of moral freedom. Human beings are not automatons or robots—they are free. God in His omnipotence allows His special creations to choose their own course, which shows how much He Himself values them. So trials—or even temptations—should not discourage us, but bring us joy. "When you are greatly tested," someone once observed, "remember God is not trying to break you; He is trying to make you."

The first Christian love is the ideal and God-approved love (Rev. 2:4). The Song of Solomon pictures such love. The book is a collection of love poems spoken alternately by a man and a woman. In a spiritual sense the lover is Jesus, the object of His love the church or the believer. "Come then, my love; my darling, come with me" (chap. 2:13, T.E.V.), Jesus says to every person.

He wants every individual to enter into a love relationship with Him. For that purpose He with His blood has redeemed all of us from Satan's claims. The only thing that can render His redemption ineffective is a perverse human will. Despite His omnipotence, God has given each person free moral choice, with the consequence that only those who choose to respond to His call will be drawn into a bond of love with Him.

Whether we realize it or not, all of us by right of creation and redemption belong to God. "You are not your own; you were bought at a price" (1 Cor. 6:19, 20). "For you know that it was not with perishable things such as silver or gold that you were redeemed from the empty way of life handed down to you from your forefathers, but with the precious blood of Christ, a lamb without blemish or defect" (1 Peter 1:18, 19). Every one of us should know that "I belong to my lover [Jesus], and his desire is for me" (S. of Sol. 7:10).

The gospel tries to convey this fact to every person. Some are unaware of it. Satan has tried to convince men ever since the Fall that the Father hates sinners. But that is a lie. He loves sinners, and because of His love for us sinners, He gave His Son to redeem us from Satan's bondage.

The love that should ideally bind a believer to Jesus is completely loyal and all-absorbing. And it is mutual. Its possessors respond readily to the slightest hints of the Partner's desires. Faith, trust, and commitment each to the other characterize it. No other lover or love can deflect their attention. Their dedication to each other is wholehearted, sincere, and genuine. No one can intrude into such a union. And it leads the believer to glad-hearted and joyous surrender.

The love of a father and mother for their children and that of a child for its parents offers another illustration. Enoch and his son Methuselah represent such a happy father-son relationship. The patriarch loved his son, and Methuselah loved and trusted his father. Through their father-son experience, Enoch gained a deeper insight into God's love and interest in him. His young son helped him to understand God better than he had before. He enjoyed working, walking, and talking with his child. In time he realized that his feelings and attitude toward Methuselah must reflect God's toward him.

"After the birth of his first son, Enoch reached a higher experience; he was drawn into a closer relationship with God. He realized more fully his own obligations and responsibility as a son of God. And as he saw the child's love for its father, its simple trust in his protection; as he felt the deep, yearning tenderness of his own heart for that firstborn son, he learned a precious lesson of the wonderful love of God to men in the gift of His Son, and the confidence which the children of God may repose in their heavenly Father. The infinite, unfathomable love of God through Christ became the subject of his meditation day and night; and with all the fervor of his soul he sought to reveal that love to the people among whom he dwelt."[3] For Enoch it was sheer joy to walk and talk with God, for God was his best friend (see Gen. 5:24).

For decades on college campuses, I have noticed how two people of the opposite sex repeatedly find occasion to walk together from one building to another across campus between classes. They enjoy and covet the company of their special friend. So Enoch's joy of being with his special Friend towered above every other desire and consideration. The two were such good friends that they did not want to part. And so God took Enoch to His home to be with Him forever. Young people do the same. They become such fast friends that they decide never to part. And so they get married.

A deep and lasting friendship developed between Enoch and God, and friendship is always of grace—a gift. It is never earned. Any relationship entered into through a monetary exchange or mutual pledges of doing something for the other individual is not a true friendship. Rather it begins with one party extending the gift of friendship or of help to another. One person extends a favor to the other. God held out his grace—His free gift of love and salvation—to Enoch as He does to every person born into our world. As a result, the gift evokes a response, and the beauty of mutual friendship wakens and grows. Nobody ever acquires true friendship through demand.

Paul's friendship with God and Jesus was so intimate that in a sense they had become one. And so Paul could joyously exclaim when he wrote to the Galatians, "Christ lives in me" (chap. 2:20). Christ in me is the wonder-working power of a personal relationship, or attachment, to the living Christ. The apostle's friendship with Christ held him steady at all times and under all circumstances. Such a pervasive relationship will bring victory to a tempted individual even where moralism usually fails. Awareness of God's presence ensures victory. The psalmist spoke from personal experience, "I am always aware of the Lord's presence; he is near, and nothing can shake me" (Ps. 16:8, T.E.V.).

In a spiritual sense Paul had died and been buried with Christ in baptism. He was dead to all that prevented complete commitment to Him and His work. But his death to self and its desires was not only once in the past. It was contemporary, continual. "I die daily" (1 Cor.

15:31, K.J.V.). His resurrection with Christ had resulted in a new life in which his will had become voluntarily captive to the mind of Christ. Through his death and resurrection with Christ, Paul had come to share the motives, purposes, and the way of Christ's self-sacrificing life.

But through the death-and-resurrection experience with Jesus, Paul had not become identified, merged, or absorbed within Him. He retained his own personality. Christ and Paul were still two distinct persons. Paul's oneness with Jesus contained no trace of pantheism. He retained freedom and responsibility to make his own decisions, but he chose to let the mind of Christ constantly guide him in shaping them. When Jesus came into his heart, he began to share His attitude toward both God and men. In body he was still "in the flesh" (Gal. 2:20, K.J.V.), living among men, but by faith he was intimately joined to Jesus.

Luther comments on the latter part of Galatians 2:20: "'Therefore,' says Paul, 'whatever this life is that I now live in the flesh, I live by faith in the Son of God.' That is, the Word I speak physically is not the word of the flesh; it is the Word of the Holy Spirit and of Christ. The vision that enters or leaves my eyes does not come from the flesh; that is, my flesh does not direct it, but the Holy Spirit does. Thus hearing does not come from the flesh, even though it is in the flesh; but it is in and from the Holy Spirit."[4]

There is not, and never has been, any other way of proving that the gospel is true and right than that of believers' daily living in accordance with the mind of Christ. That is really what Luther is saying. And Paul chose to abide in Christ.

By enticing Adam and Eve into sin, Satan for a time frustrated God's purpose for man. But not permanently. Through the plan of salvation God's desire for everyone who accepts it will ultimately be fulfilled. Consequently

Paul said that he would boast about nothing else but the cross (chap. 6:14). (The Judaizers, however, gloried in circumcision and all the rituals, rites, and ordinances of the Mosaic law.)

To Paul the cross was a constant source of joy. He knew that only through it did he have any chance of forgiveness. On the cross Jesus died in his stead. When the apostle wrote to the Corinthians, he also affirmed, "I determined to know nothing among you except Jesus Christ, and Him crucified" (1 Cor. 2:2, N.A.S.B.). To Paul, and to everyone who hopes to be saved, the cross is the only way of salvation.

But such joy and peace can flow only from a person's constant awareness that God knows his whereabouts and situation and permits adversity only because it will ultimately contribute to his good. In other words, joy in the Lord is possible only for a person who trusts Him implicitly. "Through a lack of faith, many who seek to obey the commandments of God have little peace and joy. . . . They are not anchored in Christ. Many feel a lack in their experience; they desire something which they have not."[5]

A widower with two small children hired a housekeeper. Liking the two children—a girl of 5 and a boy of 7—the woman saw to it that they were well fed, wore clean clothes, had a comfortable and well-ordered home, and were as happy as they could be without their mother. It was part of her duty as a housekeeper. For her faithful work she received a monthly salary.

After a year and a half she married their father and became their stepmother. No longer did she receive a monthly wage, but she cared for them just as gladly. Now she did it from love for both their father and them. She had enjoyed her job in the home before, but after her marriage to her former employer she was even happier. No longer did she work for him; now she was part of the family.

As members of the family of God, or church, we do not serve God as a duty. What we do is not from a sense of obligation, or because we are expected to. We do His will because we love His will and way. "For the love of Christ leaves us no choice" (2 Cor. 5:14, N.E.B.). Whether the Christian life for you and me is a burden or a privilege, a shackling restriction or freedom, a dismal journey or a honeymoon, depends on our relationship with Jesus. If you and I are married to Him, then the Christian life for us is a joy. No longer do we labor for wages as servants under the law. Instead, we belong to Him and derive pleasure from being with Him and working with Him.

After a brief honeymoon a young man prepared to take his bride to another part of the country, away from her friends and the pleasant climate where she had spent all her prior life. When I asked her whether she did not dread leaving shirt-sleeve weather for a climate where the temperature might drop down to −20° F., she instantly replied, "More than anything else I want to be where my husband is." A few months later I saw her again and inquired what she thought of the cold part of the country. "I like it here and really enjoy it," she said without hesitation. What she really meant, I believe, was that she enjoyed being with her husband. And inasmuch as he happened to work in the region, she too liked it. It was actually love for him that made the new place enjoyable for her.

Only force can occasionally make a person with an unspiritual, or carnal, mind seem to live by the will of God. For an unspiritual person, doing His will is the most oppressive yoke of bondage, slavery of the most cruel sort. Some nominal Christians find themselves in this unpleasant situation. To them Christianity is nothing but an almost unbearable burden. On every side they encounter "Don't do this," "You must not do that," "You cannot do that." They are inside the fence of God's love, but like some of the unruly heifers my family had on our small farm when I was a boy, they are continually trying to break through or push it down. And the fence of God's love is His law. Such people feel trapped inside it. While they may do merciful deeds, they do not love mercy. They may give all they possess to the poor, but as long as love does not prompt their good deeds, all is in vain (1 Cor. 13:3; Micah 6:8).

As you and I learn to know Jesus as our Saviour, Friend, and heavenly Groom, we will begin to relate to Him and His will in willing joyfulness. Details of Christian living that once might have appeared burdensome change from duties to privileges. No longer is it a pain to pay tithe and give offerings. It is an honor to help build His kingdom with the means He has entrusted to us. Instead of perhaps complaining about the burdens, privations, and the sacrifices we have to make as His followers, we will joyfully do all we can for Him and His kingdom. And when we have done that, we will wish we could do more, just as parents provide for their children and then wish they had more to give them. We shall try to ferret out God's desires as we do those of our loved ones. Our attitude will be not to ask how little we can do and still remain His, but rather how much. Gladly we shall accept Him as our Friend and Intercessor at the throne of God, and also as our King and Ruler in our daily decision-making. Acknowledging Him as the Proclaimer of God's will to us, we shall find it our joy to learn His will that we may follow it, because "the will, refined and sanctified, will find its highest delight in doing His service."[6]

One man, looking back on his life, wrote to a friend in despair, "It is too late for me now to accomplish anything in my life. I feel that the parade has passed me by. There is nothing I can do about it. I have to accept what I am."

No one freed from the burden of sin and guilt by the shed blood of Jesus, no one who is a member of the family of God, can ever feel that the parade has left him behind. Rather, he is in the parade, marching toward his heavenly home, "surrounded by such a great cloud of witnesses" (Heb. 12:1). As a follower of Jesus he is cheerful and excited, but has not yet reached the zenith of joy. That moment will commence when the parade ends on the sea of glass and every overcomer joins in the victory "song of Moses the servant of God and the song of the Lamb" (Rev. 15:3). But even now anticipation of that event thrills him. Hope sustains him, and as Emil Brunner said, "What oxygen is for the lungs such is hope for the meaning of life." For the Christian life does have meaning and overflows with hope and joy.

Thoreau said, "Surely joy is the condition of life." It is also the foretaste of life eternal. So every true follower of God possesses joy. "The genuineness, nay the actual existence, of religious experience is to be measured, not by any transcendency of feeling nor by great deeds that all men can see, but by the joy and the peace which are diffused through the soul that can say 'My Father.'"[7] Thus it is true of God's people today as it was in the time of Nehemiah, when he said to the returned captives, "'The joy of the Lord is your strength'" (Neh. 8:10).

---

[1] From O. F. Blackwelder, in *The Interpreter's Bible*, vol. 10, p. 472. Used by permission of Abingdon Press.

[2] A. T. Robertson, *Word Pictures in the New Testament*, Vol. IV, p. 12.

[3] Ellen G. White, *Patriarchs and Prophets*, p. 84.

[4] Jaroslav Pelikan (ed.), *Luther's Works*, vol. 26, p. 171.

[5] Ellen G. White, *Evangelism* (Washington, D.C.: Review and Herald Pub. Assn., 1946), p. 599.

[6] ———, *The Desire of Ages*, p. 668.

[7] Adolf Harnack, *What is Christianity?* trans. T. B. Saunders (New York: Harper & Row, 1957, first published in 1900), p. 66.

Christian Fruit-bearing

On the basis of Paul's letter to the Galatians and James's Epistle, we have briefly discussed in the preceding chapters how a sinner can be justified before God and made fit for heavenly society. As we read the two apparently contradictory letters to the church, we must keep in mind the different situations the two writers faced. Paul in Galatians—and later in Romans—combated legalism. He tried to disabuse the Galatians of the notion that they could make themselves righteous, or put themselves right with God, by their own deeds. Instead their salvation rested on faith in Jesus and in what He did for them on Calvary. James campaigned against a sterile orthodoxy that mouthed a faith that produced no results. His readers tended to turn God's mercy into a cheap grace with freedom from the Christian discipline and fruitful action that naturally flow from a converted person's knowledge of God's will.

Saving faith and works have no conflict with each other. They are always good neighbors, always live together, are inextricably linked one to the other. Joseph Beaumont says that "faith and works are like the light and heat of a candle; they cannot be separated." The one is not a rival to the other. Rather, faith is the dynamic that produces works in conformity with God's will. Without action, faith is but pretention. The noted news commentator Paul Harvey once stated that he thinks "of faith as the horse and of works as the cart, that one without the other is impotent." He continued by saying that he felt that "a man who takes John 3:16 without taking 1 John 2:3, 'Hereby we do know that we know him, if we keep his commandments,' . . . is a fraud and a fake and is trying to drive two horses going in opposite directions."[1]

Paul and James were but the first of countless Christian writers to confront the difficulty of giving a short but balanced presentation of God's grace and man's visible response prompted by new life within. Luther also met it. Commenting on the Epistle to the Galatians, he wrote: "It is difficult and dangerous to teach that we are justified by faith without works and yet to require works at the same time. Unless the ministers of Christ are faithful and prudent here and are 'stewards of the mysteries of God' (1 Cor. 4:1), who rightly divide the Word of truth (2 Tim. 2:15), they will immediately confuse faith and love at this point. Both topics, faith and works, must be carefully taught and emphasized, but in such a way that they both remain within their limits. Otherwise, if works alone are taught, as happened under the papacy, faith is lost. If faith alone is taught, unspiritual men will immediately suppose that works are not necessary."[2]

He noted further that "if we teach faith, carnal people will neglect works; but if we urge works, faith and the comfort of consciences will be lost."[3]

Ellen G. White says that "the apostle James saw that dangers would arise in presenting the subject of justification by faith, and he labored to show that genuine faith cannot exist without corresponding works. The experience of Abraham is presented. 'Seest thou,' he says, 'how faith wrought with his works, and by works was faith made perfect?' Thus genuine faith does a genuine work in the believer. Faith and obedience bring a solid, valuable experience. . . . The so-called faith that does not work by love and purify the soul will not justify any man."[4]

A knowledgeable physician does not give the same treatment to all his patients. He prescribes the medicine that will alleviate the suffering and cure the ailment of each. His remedies differ with each case. And the same is true of physicians of the soul. Both Paul and James were guided by the Master Physician, Jesus, who knows each believer (see Rev. 2:2-6) and gives him what he needs. For example, Jesus chided His hearers on different occasions for their lack of faith. To the disciples He said, "'O you of little faith!'" (Luke 12:28); to Peter when sinking into the water, "'You of little faith'" (Matt. 14:31); to the multitudes worrying about food and clothing, "'O you of little faith'" (chap. 6:30). But to the rich young ruler He did not urge faith. Instead He tried to stir him to action. "'Go, sell,'" He requested (chap. 19:21).

Through the Holy Spirit, Jesus guided the apostles to prescribe for each group of believers what they needed. Thus Paul emphasized faith for those who gloried in an abundance of works of righteousness but lacked saving faith. On the other hand, James prescribed action, commensurate with their alleged faith, for those who believed but failed to do.

True Christianity is action. In the Sermon on the Mount, Jesus asked, "'What are you doing more than others?'" (chap. 5:47). Jesus is interested not in dead belief, but in action-producing faith. "'Not everyone who says to me, "Lord, Lord," will enter the kingdom of heaven, but only he who does the will of my Father who is in heaven'" (chap. 7:21).

James, as surely as Paul, believed that faith is

necessary for personal justification, as we pointed out in Chapter VIII. And Paul knew that justifying faith will produce works. He went so far as to say that the only thing that really "matters is faith that works through love" (Gal. 5:6, T.E.V.), and "it is not those who hear the law who are righteous in God's sight, but it is those who obey the law who will be declared righteous" (Rom. 2:13). Christ's imputed righteousness does not, according to Paul, free a believer from future obedience to God's law. To the Corinthians Paul admonished, "For whether or not a man is circumcised means nothing; what matters is to obey God's commandments" (1 Cor. 7:19, T.E.V.). Paul recognized, as Lenski put it, that "the one who is justified will ever live as a result of the faith by which he is justified."[5]

But "to rely on 'works of law' is never to have justification. . . . To produce 'works' [of faith] is to have justification, for their absence shows that a faith which we claim to have is dead and barren (James 2:17, 20), their presence that faith is faith indeed, alive, embracing Christ, and thus full of good works. The devils believe, are they justified (James 2:19)."[6]

"The verdict on that faith [that produces no action response] is condemnation since such a faith could embrace Christ only outwardly. Every *subsequent* verdict that finds us with the works of faith acquits us, declares us righteous, for the works of faith attest the genuineness of the faith which inwardly and truly clings to Christ."[7]

Having been put into a right relationship with God, or justified, a person will do good deeds. "The doers of the law," said Luther, "are believers, who, having received the Holy Spirit, fulfill the law and love God and their neighbor. Thus the 'doer of the law' . . . is one who, having already become a person through faith, then becomes a doer. . . . Those who have been made righteous do righteous things. . . . Therefore we, being justified by faith, do good works, through which, as 2 Peter 1:10 says, our call and election are confirmed and made more certain day by day."[8]

"Therefore 'to do' is first to believe and so, through faith, to keep the law. For we must receive the Holy Spirit; illumined and renewed by Him, we begin to keep the law, to love God and our neighbor."[9] Indeed, if Abraham and Sarah had just believed in God's power and promise of a son but had not acted on their faith, Isaac would never have been born. But Abraham and Sarah's saving faith made them act. Their response showed their faith. "The word of God is against this ensnaring doctrine of faith without works."[10] If we as Christians have nothing more than what the demons have—"the devils have faith" (James 2:19, N.E.B.)—then both we and our faith are in bad shape. "Pure doctrine will blend with works of righteousness; heavenly precepts will mingle with holy practices."[11]

Both the dangers that Paul and James faced lurk still in today's church. Our culture is not preoccupied with amassing good deeds. Even many who believe in God seem to take His approval upon their lives and deeds for granted while they spend their time and money solely on their own needs and pleasures. Knowing that God is a God of love, they also assume that He is indulgent. Hence, they worship an indulgent God who in His love overlooks and tolerates almost any violation of His expressed will and condones anything they choose to do. With unsubdued drive to gratify indwelling sin, they still claim security in the shed blood of Christ. Few speak or think of a God who transforms human lives into the likeness of a Jesus who denied His human desires and did the will of His Father for the salvation of sinners. On the other side, some self-confident Christians almost think they merit or can earn their salvation by their righteous living.

James speaks for God to the first group. In his letter

he points out their failings. Rather than being an "epistle of straw," as Luther termed it, it is an Epistle of rock to us and to our generation. It breaks to pieces our comfortable illusions of discipleship that demand neither sacrifice of time or means nor change of attitude or behavior. The book candidly tells us how our foolishness has led us to think that belief and behavior have nothing in common. He makes it plain that there is to be a noticeable difference between a Christian and a non-Christian. "You fool!" he shouts to us. "Do you want to be shown that faith without actions is useless?" (chap. 2:20, T.E.V.), or "But can you not see, you quibbler, that faith divorced from deeds is barren?" (N.E.B.). Through his letter James summons us back to a love relationship with God that changes those He loves into thankful and obedient disciples—to a discipleship that costs something rather than just making us feel good. Jesus' followers should show the fruits of the gospel in Christian doing. Paul, on the other hand, in Galatians reminds us that acceptable Christian doing will spring from Christians who have accepted Jesus and His merits as the only basis for their justification and salvation.

Luther wrote: "Insist on it, then, that inwardly, in the spirit, before God, man is justified through faith alone, without all works, but outwardly and publicly, before the people and himself, he is justified through works, that is, he thereby becomes known and certain himself that he honestly believes and is pious. Therefore you may call the one a public justification, the other an inward justification, but in this sense that the public justification is only a fruit, a result, and a proof of the justification in the heart. Accordingly, man is not justified by it before God but must previously be justified before Him. Just so you may call the fruits of the tree the obvious goodness of the tree, which follows and proves its inner, natural goodness.

"This is what St. James means in his Epistle when he says (chap. 2:26): 'Faith without works is dead,' that is, the fact that works do not follow is a certain sign that there is no faith, but dead thought and dream, which people falsely call faith." [12]

Stott observes that "the two men [Paul and James] were given a different ministry but not a different message. They proclaimed the same gospel, but with different emphasis." [13] Consequently we, as God's children today, should refrain from assigning a priority of spiritual value to either one when they comment on justification. The Holy Spirit inspired both and included their writings in the Bible "for our own instruction" (Rom. 15:4, N.E.B.), as Paul says about the Old Testament Scriptures. For that reason every faithful believer and proclaimer of God's truth finds it necessary to use both the soul-stirring teachings of Paul and the sensible, down-to-earth Epistle of James to build and nurture a saving faith.

---

[1] Ralph Blodgett, "Paul Harvey—The Rest of the Story," *These Times*, October, 1979.

[2] Jaroslav Pelikan (ed.), *Luther's Works*, vol. 27, pp. 62, 63.

[3] *Ibid.*, p. 75.

[4] *The SDA Bible Commentary*, Ellen G. White Comments, on James 2:21-26, p. 936.

[5] R. C. H. Lenski, *The Interpretation of St. Paul's Epistles to the Galatians, to the Ephesians, and to the Philippians* (Columbus, Ohio: The Wartburg Press, 1946), p. 145.

[6] ———, *The Interpretation of St. Paul's Epistle to the Romans*, (Columbus, Ohio: Wartburg Press, 1945), p. 285.

[7] ———, *The Interpretation of the Epistle to the Hebrews and the Epistle of James*, p. 589.

[8] Pelikan, *op. cit.*, vol. 26, pp. 259, 260.

[9] *Ibid.*, p. 255.

[10] Ellen G. White, *The Great Controversy*, p. 472.

[11] ———, *The Acts of the Apostles*, p. 560.

[12] Ewald M. Plass (comp.), *What Luther Says*, Vol. III, pp. 1231, 1232.

[13] John R. W. Stott, *Basic Introduction to the New Testament*, pp. 104, 105.